A
Time
for Every
Purpose

A
Time
for Every
Purpose

Bob Ricker
&
Ron Pitkin

Thomas Nelson Publishers
Nashville • Camden • New York

Published in Nashville, Tennessee, by Thomas Nelson, Inc. and distributed in Canada by Lawson Falle, Ltd., Cambridge, Ontario.

Printed in the United States of America.

Unless otherwise noted, the Bible text in this publication is from THE NEW KING JAMES Version. Copyright © 1979, 1980, 1982, Thomas Nelson, Inc. Publishers.

Scripture quotations noted KJV are from the King James Version of the Bible.

Scripture quotations noted RSV are from the Revised Standard Version of the Bible, copyrighted 1946, 1952, © 1971, 1973.

Scripture quotations noted PHILLIPS are from J. B. Phillips: THE NEW TESTA-MENT IN MODERN ENGLISH, Revised Edition. J. B. Phillips 1958, 1960, 1972. Used by permission of MacMillan Publishing Co., Inc.

The Scripture quotation from *The Living Bible* (© 1971) is used by permission of Tyndale House Publishers.

The Scripture quotation noted "Today's English Version" is from the *Good News Bible*–Old Testament: copyright © American Bible Society 1976.

ISBN 0-8407-5857-X

To my wife, Dee,
who has made Ecclesiastes 9:9 easy and fun,
and to our children, Todd and Kristen,
who have brought us unspeakable joy
and in truth are
"a heritage from the Lord"
(Ps. 127:3).

CONTENTS

ACKNOWLEDGMENTS

Long before I ever thought about studying the Book of Ecclesiastes, I had learned a great deal about its truths. My mother and father had taught them to me, largely in the course of daily life.

All during my growing-up years, I sat under my father's powerful preaching, hoping that some day God would be able to use me as He was using him. He challenged me to live for God and for eternal realities. My precious mother, a real Bible student and gifted communicator in her own right, also gave me her rich insight into life and pastoring.

I will never forget the day when she told her young preacher-son, "Bobby, if you teach the Scriptures well to your congregation and let them know you love them, they'll overlook many weaknesses." The congregations I have pastored have had their share of opportunities to prove her right!

So, thanks, Mother and Dad. You taught me where to find lasting happiness in life, and I love you for it. When God chose parents for me, He picked out the very best. And I'm so grateful, to Him and to you.

My thoughts of writing a book were on the back burner when Peter Gillquist, senior editor at Thomas Nelson Publishers, visited me. As we talked, I warmed to the idea of writing a book, and before long I was telling him how much I had enjoyed preaching through the Book of Ecclesiastes. "Great!" he exclaimed. "I love the book, too. I think you ought to share what you've learned in writing."

I had just finished the sermon series, and the dear folk of Grace Church of Edina had responded to the great and timeless themes of Ecclesiastes with enthusiasm. One man had even come to me one day to say, "You can stay in Ecclesiastes as long as you like!" Furthermore, I knew it was a book many can hardly *find* in the

Bible, much less understand. Having just finished months of study on it, I knew how contemporary and relevant it is. It is a book come of age.

With my busy schedule, I knew I did not have time to write a book. However, the Lord provided another man who has been fascinated with Ecclesiastes for many years. Before long, Ron Pitkin, reference book editor at Thomas Nelson, and I were busy writing and rewriting, traveling and corresponding between Nashville and Minneapolis.

Many thanks are due my marvelous secretary, Naomi Hendricks, who typed the various manuscript drafts and handled the busy correspondence. I am thankful for her loyalty and skill.

And many thanks to you, too, Ron, for the excellent job you did in taking the rough, verbal form and turning it into a readable, thoughtful manuscript. You have become more than a co-author and editor. You have become a good friend. Without your hard work, the book would not have been written. Working with you has been a blessing.

BOB RICKER

CHAPTER ONE
Ecclesiastes: A Book
Whose Time Has Come

I normally look at a map before venturing on a journey.

Recently, my family and I drove from Arizona to our home in Minnesota. Having misplaced my road atlas, I drove all the way home by memory. I probably should have purchased a new atlas, but I had decided to try the trip without one. In spite of a few missed turns, eventually I made it back safely. But my trip would have been much easier if I had taken the time and money necessary to buy a map.

I approach the reading of a book with that same road-map philosophy. I first turn to the introduction or first chapter, for usually a good book will give me a reliable "road map" in one of those places. It charts out the terrain over which the author wishes to take me; it expounds the benefits I will enjoy from reading it; it defines the questions it will ask and answer. In short, it tells me what to expect.

So I have prepared this introductory chapter with these questions in mind: What is this book and why should I read it? How will it help me make sense out of the Book of Ecclesiastes? And how will it help me make sense out of life?

OF LIFE AND WISDOM

The Book of Ecclesiastes is a book about life. Its writer, King Solomon, was a realist. In fact, I would even call him a realist's realist! He writes with candor about frustration, fulfillment, work, sex, injustice, friendship, worship, happiness, insecurity, suffering, temptation, folly, confusion, emptiness—our concerns. Even more importantly, he writes about these topics with a kind of brutal honesty and unsentimental clarity that even today few would dare to express in a religious book. His observations are

11

really the conclusions that life itself forces upon us—if we have the stomach for the truth.

Ecclesiastes is also a book about wisdom. Solomon writes that we need two kinds of wisdom. The first is the wisdom that tells us how to get things done in this world—*practical wisdom*. If you want to get ahead in life and want to avoid trouble, Ecclesiastes has some sound practical advice. How do things work? How can I get the most out of life? Ecclesiastes will tell you.

The second type of wisdom is God's wisdom. This *spiritual wisdom* tells us what is eternally important. True, it is wise not to whisper sedition against the king (see 10:20); it is also wise to know that God made us (see 12:1) and that He will eventually pass judgment on our lives (see 12:14). That is, it is one thing to fear the king; it is quite another to fear God. It is this kind of wisdom Solomon had in mind when he wrote, "The fear of the LORD is the beginning of wisdom" (Prov. 9:10).

IS THAT ALL THERE IS?

Do you ever get blue watching the evening news? I confess I do. In our city, like yours, crime is increasing. The legitimate poor are struggling because of new regulations brought on by welfare cheaters. A new abortion clinic is opening. The gays want rights, not repentance. I go to the monthly ministerial meeting looking for an encouraging note. It's not there. One church is going through a split. Another evangelical pastor has left his wife. Lord, what do You have to tell us?

Solomon constructs an interesting answer in Ecclesiastes. Simply put, he says that all human striving is worthless. It is not worth the puff of wind it takes to blow it away. In writing these rather strong words, "vanity of vanities, all is vanity" (1:2), I believe King Solomon had his eye on two people. First, he was looking back on his own life with remorse over his follies. Second, he was looking at the all-too-common pagan (today we call him a "secularist") who sees no reason to involve God in his life. "I do quite well without God's help, thank you." Quite successful in his own eyes, he looks down at those who believe God is important.

So Solomon decides to meet the secular person on his own ground. It is as though he says, "O.K. Let's assume that God is irrelevant. But if God is out of the picture, who's in? What does life become without Him?"

The first element he finds is *death*. Death is a rather serious problem for the person who has all his eggs in an earthly basket. Death is a fact of life that cannot be avoided. "And how does a wise man die? As the fool!" (2:16). For all we can see, that might as well be life's final verdict.

The second element Solomon finds is *evil*. He finds evil everywhere. Wickedness where justice should be executed (see 3:16), oppression of the poor in favor of the powerful (see 4:1), envy that accompanies every success (see 4:4), the greed of the wealthy (see 4:8), social systems that exploit (see 5:8), sinful men everywhere (see 7:20), and a mad thirst for evil (see 9:3)—all fill the earth. These evils, too, are easy to observe.

The third fact Solomon finds is *time and chance* (see 9:11–12). He explodes the myth that man is the master of his fate. Instead, time and chance end up getting all of us. We are like the unsuspecting fish that is rudely taken from the water when his time "falls suddenly" upon him (9:12). All of us have seen the brutal work of time and chance; we see their effects every day.

So this is what life without God is like. And having made his point, Solomon again declares, "vanity of vanities, all is vanity" (12:8). Thus Solomon both begins and ends his description of life with these bookends of despair.

NO, THERE'S MORE

But Solomon is a man of faith, and he is not willing to leave the reader in that bone-chilling condition. He cannot resist proclaiming his own faith as he rests his case:

Let us hear the conclusion of the whole matter:

Fear God and keep His commandments,
For this is the whole duty of man,
For God will bring every work into judgment,
Including every secret thing,
Whether it is good or whether it is evil (12:13–14).

Even though Ecclesiastes is filled with statements about the futility of the human experience, Solomon is too much a man of faith to hide his own beliefs. He has much to say about God, even though he uses few words to say it.

In the course of Ecclesiastes he uses five separate attributes of God to express his convictions. 1. As *Creator*, God makes all things. We are told that we "do not know the works of God who makes all things" (11:5). It is He who creates, not us; and we cannot change it. Everything has its season (see 3:1–8), and not one of us can do so much as make a crooked thing straight (see 7:13) or make the wind blow one way or another (see 11:5).

2. As *Sovereign*, God is in charge. It is God who has given a "grievous task" to mankind (1:13); it is God who "gives wisdom and knowledge and joy to a man who is good in His sight," but takes the sinner's work from him (2:26); and it is God who protects "the righteous and the wise and their works" (9:1).

3. As *Wisdom*, God is unsearchable. In 3:11 we are told, "Also He has put eternity in their hearts, except that no one can find out the work that God does from the beginning to end." In 7:14 we are also told that God has made good and bad times "so that man can find nothing that will happen after him." Furthermore, even a wise man will be unable to understand the works of God (see 7:23–24; 8:17).

4. As the *Righteous* One, God will surely judge. He will judge the wicked (see 3:17); the works of the righteous are in His hand (see 9:1); we are to live with the judgment in mind, even from the days of our youth (see 11:9); and ultimately everything and everyone will experience God's judgment (see 12:14).

5. As *Love*, God can be trusted. I believe this is what Solomon implied when he wrote:

> For I considered all this in my heart, so that I could declare it to all: that the righteous and the wise and their works are in the hand of God. People know neither love nor hatred by anything that is before them (9:1).

I do not believe that Solomon is saying that we cannot know whether God is a god of love. It is important to remember that, by inspiration of God, he is presenting his argument to the secular-minded person. It seems to me that what he says is, "O.K., for the sake of the argument, this time let's assume there is a God. But based on what we see around us—evil and suffering and death—we really can't tell whether He loves or hates us. So what is the point of talking about it?"

Of course Solomon knew that God loves us! He knew the answer to his question. For those who do not know the answer, however, it is a terrifying question. But all who know Solomon's God also know that it is a wonderful question. "Ah, yes! He loves me. That's the kind of God He is."

A FAITH-FILLED PERSPECTIVE

It would be easy to assume that a book filled with "vanity of vanities" would advocate a pinch-faced approach to life. But that is not the case. Repeatedly, Solomon declares that life is a gift from God, and we are to live it with joy (see 2:24–25; 3:13; 5:18–20; 8:15; 9:7–9; 11:9). Certainly, in view of his keen awareness of the dark side of life, his is a remarkable, faith-filled perspective. We who are blessed with so much would do well to learn of joy and gratitude from him.

As I study the Book of Ecclesiastes, I find it to be a practical and reliable guide to twentieth-century life. Time and again I have been amazed at how accurately Solomon described the world. It never fails to overwhelm me that in spite of its surface cynicism, the message of Ecclesiastes is as reliable and hope-filled in our modern, secular age as it was when first penned thousands of years ago. That is why I love this book.

Come, walk through it with me.

CHAPTER TWO

Why Does My Life Seem So Pointless?

Ecclesiastes 1:1–11

He was a brilliant man. Those who knew him well and those who only knew him by reputation said he had more than just raw intelligence. He was able to *use* what he knew. He was wise.

And yet, as I read his story, I thought of how incredibly foolish he had been. Born into wealth and power, he had been raised with all the advantages they offer. He had enjoyed the best education money could buy. Loved by his father, King David, he was handpicked to be his successor.

As he followed in his father's steps, success followed upon success. His accomplishments even outdid his father's. It was not long, however, before he slipped into an all-too-familiar pattern. He became involved with one new woman, then another. Then many. Soon he abandoned the principles by which both he and his father had expanded their holdings. He became harsh and arbitrary in his decisions. He drifted away from God and the principles he had been taught as a child.

He simply lost his way.

As I continued to follow his story, I learned that eventually he returned to those basic convictions of his youth. He saw how foolish a wise man can be when he takes his eyes off God. So he repented of his foolishness and his sin. And his willingness to turn from dissolute pleasure-seeking to serving God and man caused his reputation as a wise man to spread far and wide.

His name? King Solomon of Israel.

I believe it was sometime late in his life—perhaps as he sat reflecting on the folly of his younger years—that he resolved to use his God-given insight and intelligence to show us all how life really is and how to better navigate through it.

Not life as the image-makers and manipulators want us to see it, mind you. Not life as the users and exploiters want us to view it.

Not life as those who have a stake in our not thinking clearly want us to feel about it.

No. Solomon wanted to paint a picture of the truth that all could see, in his day and in ours. He wanted everyone to know exactly what life holds for the person who has no use for God, or who talks as if he does but ignores Him. He also wanted everyone to know exactly what life will be like for those who love the Lord, learn justice and mercy, and walk humbly before God. No sentiment. No punches pulled. Just the truth.

So he wrote a book. We call it the Book of Ecclesiastes, which is its title in the Greek version of the Old Testament. In Hebrew the title is *Qoheleth,* which can mean either one who collects wise sayings or one who speaks to an assembly—"The Preacher," as many versions translate it.

He wasted little time getting to the point of his message. And when he began, he sounded like a battle-worn cynic who had lost his capacity for joy.

The words of the Preacher, the son of David, king in Jerusalem.

"Vanity of vanities," says the Preacher;
"vanity of vanities, all is vanity" (1:1–2).

This certainly does not sound like what we might expect to hear from a man who is about to challenge us to live for God! His words sound more like the cynical counsel of a much later philosopher from France, named Camus, who said that life is a bad joke.

Solomon's observations about life, however, will not turn out false or depressing. As one reads through Ecclesiastes, it is the *realism* of his words that is striking. They take on a tone of brutal honesty.

What Solomon seems to be doing throughout this short book is showing us what life is like from two distinct points of view—from the one who fears the Lord and from the one who does not. But he plays the game by the secularist's rules. He shows us what life is like when we consider only the evidence that our senses give us.

"Vanity of vanities, all is vanity." Why "vanity"? The word means "vapor, breath"—something transitory and unsubstantial. You cannot grasp breath. It eludes you.

If all you can believe in is what you can see and touch and prove, and if all you can prove about life is that it is here and then it is gone, then everything is like vapor or breath.

So far Solomon has only asserted his thesis. As we continue reading, we see that he does not shrink from its implications. He looks at four areas of life—work, nature, the senses, history—to see what they might teach about the meaning of life.

WORK

Several years ago when I was in my twenties, a friend and I decided we needed some additional income. We began to look for a car in bad repair that could be bought cheap, fixed up, and sold for a good profit. It took little time to find a car in bad repair! We named it the Blue Ox, for obvious reasons, and began our work on it as soon as it was ours.

As we repaired one defect, we would find something else that needed work. Our investment became increasingly expensive. Finally, after several weeks' work, we were ready to sell the Blue Ox and make our fortunes.

We ran our ad in the newspaper, but to no avail.

Finally, we had to lower our price, and eventually we sold the car. When we sat down that night to pay off our bills and total the amount we had gained, each of us had a profit of $35.00! We learned a good lesson about old cars and fast dollars, but we had very little gain.

Have you seen the television commerical where a bright young man in a three-piece suit admits to the viewers, "I am making more money now than I ever have. But I have nothing to show for it."? Ever feel that way? Solomon did. He knew all about working hard and coming up empty-handed.

What profit has a man from all his labor
In which he toils under the sun?
One generation passes away, and another generation comes;
But the earth abides forever (1:3–4).

When Solomon uses the word "profit" here, he is using it in the same way we do. It is a Hebrew word taken from the ancient business world, and it means money gained from work rendered.

"When I've done my work, what's left for me?" We all understand
that question. It is a fair one. Even Jesus used the same imagery
when He asked, "For what will it profit a man if he gains the whole
world, and loses his own soul?" (Mark 8:36).

When he uses the word *toil*, Solomon is speaking of hard labor.
No air-conditioned offices, company cars, or any of the other modern perks here! Since the fall of man, we have been called to toil (see
Gen. 3:17–19). The command, "Six days you shall labor" comes
before "the seventh day is the Sabbath. . . . In it you shall do no
work" (Ex. 20:9–10). We need to worship God, and we need to
work. Both are important.

But what is the point of our toil? Verse 4 adds the next dark
stroke: "One generation passes away, and another generation
comes; but the earth abides forever." The word *earth* means the dirt
on which we walk. It outlasts us! We, who are made in the image of
God and are the pinnacle of His creation, will be survived by the
very dirt from which we are molded. This has happened for generations; it will happen to us.

So what do we accomplish when we go to the office—or wherever we go—to do whatever toil is ours? And what is our toil going
to mean? What is the gain? What is the profit? When the transac-
tion is over, when all the taxes and Social Security and hospitaliza-
tion insurance and retirement benefits have been withheld, what
do I take home?

> Then I looked on all the works that my hands had done
> And on the labor in which I had toiled;
> And indeed all was vanity and grasping for the wind.
> There was no profit under the sun (2:11).

No profit. No gain. Solomon had spent so much of his life
chasing the wind. "It was all vanity!" he concludes. Who ever really
catches the wind? Who ever grasps everything he wants? And even
if we are fortunate enough to amass a fortune from our toil, over the
long run our efforts are still futile.

> As he came from his mother's womb, naked shall he return,
> To go as he came;
> And he shall take nothing from his labor
> Which he may carry away in his hand (5:15).

We came into this world with nothing; we will be just as rich when we leave it. Then why are we engaged in this feverish activity, especially when in the end it turns out like the Blue Ox?

That is life's verdict for the secularist who faces the implications of what he believes. We live. We work. We die. And the beat goes on.

But wait a minute! How about us who believe, who inhabit the kingdom of God? Solomon forces the Christian to look at his work and ask what the profit is. Is there any eternal gain that can accrue to our toil? Surely there must be a godly motive in hauling off to work each day.

FOUR OBJECTIVES FOR OUR WORK

Let me suggest four reasons why we should work. First, *we work to bring glory to God.* "Whatever you do, do all to the glory of God" (1 Cor. 10:31). The quality of our work, the integrity with which we do it, and the love we show while doing it—all can bring glory to God.

One of the most effective glorifiers of God I ever knew was a parking-lot attendant at a well-known restaurant. An elderly gentleman, he served his customers with more grace and enthusiasm than many of us exude who pastor churches. Another was a lady who made wedding cakes for a living in her home kitchen. Not only her demeanor, but the artistry and quality of her work spoke of the order of the kingdom. So, let us glorify God in *everything* we do, even in tasks that the world may call mundane.

Second, *we work to gain a livelihood.* "If anyone will not work, neither shall he eat" (2 Thess. 3:10). There is a joy in meeting life's basic needs through work. It is God's plan, and we are privileged to be a part of it.

Third, *we work to have wealth to share.* "Let him labor, working with his hands what is good, that he may have something to give to him who has need" (Eph. 4:28). Giving makes our work sacred. Why? Because when we give, we are following God's example (see John 3:16).

Tragically, one of the prime vices of the day—even among Christians—is greed. How can you combat it? The most effective way I know is by almsgiving, doling out of our abundance to those in need. Look for ways, watch for opportunities to share with the poor the excess of your wealth. One friend has a habit of keeping an eye out for young married couples whose shoestring budgets do not allow them to have an occasional evening out. He delights in putting twenty-five or thirty dollars in an envelope—anonymously if possible—and sending them out to dinner.

Another friend bought a dog and gave him to a man down the street who is lonely because he lives alone. With tears of gratitude, the neighbor received his warm and wiggling gift. Be creative as you watch for ways to express your gratitude to God.

Fourth, *we work to have bridges for Christian witness.* Jesus told us to make disciples while we live (see Matt. 28:19). Most of us have many opportunities to share Christ with the people we know.

One of the great advantages a lay man or woman has over those in full-time pastoral work in the area of Christian witness is *natural contact* with nonbelievers. People in normal daily working or neighborhood relationships have unforced friendships that a pastor can rarely develop.

A friend served for several years on the staff of a campus ministry. Later he accepted an administrative post at a large university. Referring to his period of employment at the university he said: "They were the richest years of evangelism I ever had. I was not 'paid' to talk about Christ. I witnessed within the system, not simply to the system."

Don't despair because your responsibilities as a wife, mother, plumber, or insurance agent limit your time for Christian service. What you may lose in *hours* available, you more than make up for in *lives* available. Take heart! You're out where the people are!

When it is done for the Lord, a Christian's work is sacred. We are not just working for money. We cannot take it with us anymore than the unbeliever can take his with him. We are not working for power or luxury. We labor to give glory to God, to sustain our lives, to be able to help others, and to build bridges for winning and discipling people to Him.

NATURE

God's creation gives our lives incredible stability and continuity. Several months ago, for example, my wife and I returned to where we had spent our honeymoon. We visited the mountain streams where we had sat eighteen years earlier. We have both changed during those eighteen years, but the streams have not. Eighteen years or eighteen hundred years have not made any appreciable difference.

In like manner, we enjoy the variety of seasons in Minnesota. In the fall I look forward to the snow covering my lawn so I will not have to mow the grass, and the cold so I will not have to repaint the house. In the winter I look forward to spring when it will be warm and we can play golf and tennis and cook out-of-doors. In the spring I look forward to the summer so I can be with my family, do a little fishing and traveling, or sit by a lake for quiet reflection. (I also try to convince myself that it is wiser to paint the house in the fall than in the spring.) In the summer I look forward to fall when things get back on schedule and the weather cools.

Solomon understood these movements of nature, and he knew that long after we have left this earth the forces of nature will continue on in their predictable ways.

> The sun also rises, and the sun goes down,
> And hastens to the place where it arose.
> The wind goes toward the south,
> And turns around to the north;
> The wind whirls about continually,
> And comes again on its circuit.
> All the rivers run into the sea,
> Yet the sea is not full;
> To the place from which the rivers come,
> There they return again (1:5–7).

Keep in mind that Solomon is showing us how nature works, and he is doing so from the point of view of someone who ignores the Lord. To a person who is not honest enough to face the fact that God made all this, nature *is* pointless. The sun rises only to set again. The wind blows from one direction, then another; but eventually it gets back to where it was. The streams keep running to the same places, and those places never get full; their sources never run dry.

So what is the point? Nature has been going its way for a long time, and it will continue to do so long after we are gone. That is all the secularist can ever say about the subject and remain "objective."

The believer, on the other hand, discovers great meaning in nature.

At sunrise or sunset I can be reminded to praise the Lord for His blessings. "From the rising of the sun to its going down/The LORD's name is to be praised" (Ps. 113:3).

As I sit by the stream or river, I can let my soul be challenged. "As the deer pants for the water brooks,/So pants my soul for You, O God" (Ps. 42:1).

I can rejoice in the drama of that storm, for my Lord is master of even the fiercest elements of nature. "He [Jesus] arose and rebuked the wind, and said to the sea, 'Peace, be still!' And the wind ceased and there was a great calm. . . . And they feared exceedingly, and said one to another, 'Who can this be, that even the wind and the sea obey Him?'" (Mark 4:39, 41).

When I look into space and see the vast galaxies that make our sun and earth seem so small, I can marvel at His love for me. "But the very hairs of your head are all numbered" (Matt. 10:30).

When I see the beauty of this earth, I can know that the same One who made it is preparing another place for me. "And if I go and prepare a place for you, I will come again and receive you to Myself; that where I am, there you may be also" (John 14:3).

When I see the birds and flowers, I know that God has provided for them, and His provision for me is much greater.

"Look at the birds of the air, for they neither sow nor reap nor gather into barns; yet your heavenly Father feeds them. Are you not of more value than they? . . . Consider the lilies of the field, how they grow: they neither toil nor spin; and yet I say to you that even Solomon in all his glory was not arrayed like one of these" (Matt. 6:26, 28–29).

Without a knowledge of the Lord Jesus Christ, everything in nature is so pointless. Season follows season, but nothing really changes. But to one who sees life from God's perspective, nature is full of value for time and eternity.

THE SENSES

Solomon continues his probing. This time he takes a look at two of our most important senses—sight and hearing.

All things are full of labor;
Man cannot express it.
The eye is not satisfied with seeing,
Nor the ear filled with hearing (1:8).

I have often thanked the Lord that I have good sight and hearing. And yet this Preacher complains that even those two senses are so filled with weariness that he cannot describe it all. Why? Because the eye is never satisfied, no matter how much it sees or how much we possess. And the ear can never hear all it wants, especially of those things that please it.

Several years ago a popular singer expressed much the same sentiment, only in a completely secular sense. She sang of young love, pleasure, marriage, children, and even life and death. At the end of each stanza, she would lament her hopeless cry that if that was all there is, then we should just get drunk and have a good time. Presumably, no matter how good something is, it is not enough. Life is just a series of disappointing experiences.

A person who does not have Christ at the center of life can never be truly satisfied. Regardless of how much he sees or hears, owns or experiences, it is never enough. There will always be that craving for more. Why? *Because there is an empty spot in our lives that only God can fill.* No amount of activity or success can ever fill it in His absence.

The psalmist writes, "Delight yourself also in the LORD,/And He shall give you the desires of your heart" (Ps. 37:4). God has reserved the privilege of bringing satisfaction and meaning to our lives for Himself. We will not find it anywhere else.

HISTORY

You have heard it before: "There is nothing new under the sun." Look who said it first.

> That which has been is what will be,
> That which is done is what will be done,
> And there is nothing new under the sun.
> Is there anything of which it may be said, "See, this is new"?
> It has already been in ancient times before us (1:9–10).

The French have a proverb that goes, "The more things change, the more they turn out to be the same." That is what Solomon means. He is not saying that people never invent anything new or that every object on the face of the earth is exactly as it always has been. That would be a ridiculous belief. Instead, Solomon is offering a sweeping comment on life. It is as if he is saying, "No matter how much we think we've changed things, the old ways still go on."

"That which has been is what will be. . . . Is there anything of which it may be said, 'See, this is new?' It has already been." Solomon, remember, is building his case; and this time he is showing secular man the emptiness of his life in view of the sweep of history. What has happened in the past was not unique, and neither is what is happening today.

This pointlessness extends to all history, the past and the future. Some hope to pin their hopes for meaning on the dream that they will be remembered after they die, a sort of immortality in others' minds. Listen to Solomon's warning.

> There is no remembrance of former things,
> Nor will there be any remembrance of things that are to come
> By those who will come after (1:11).

Mankind is not particularly interested in the past. We know some of what has gone before us, but very little of it has become a part of our memory. It has little meaning for most of us. Historians remind us of this, saying that human beings have benefited very little from the mistakes of the past. So all we learn from history is that we learn nothing from history. Similarly, it is foolish to think that future generations will be standing in line to join our fan clubs!

How pointless our lives seem in the light of history. Unless. . . .

When Solomon uses the phrase "under the sun" (he uses it thirty times in Ecclesiastes), he is talking about the observable world. He is not talking about spiritual or eternal things. He is talking about the things that are important to those who live their lives believing that what they experience on earth is all there is.

Solomon is building his case with these words. Soon he will tell us what his point is, but it will not be found in the meaningless cycle of each generation reliving the story and repeating the mistakes of previous generations.

WHEN GOD IS AT WORK

The truth is that there are new things. All of them come from the hands of a loving God.

He has put a new song in my mouth—
Praise to our God;
Many will see it and fear,
And will trust in the LORD (Ps. 40:3).

"For behold, I create new heavens and a new earth" (Is. 65:17).

"Then I will give them one heart, and I will put a new spirit within them, and take the stony heart out of their flesh, and give them a heart of flesh" (Ezek. 11:19).

Therefore, if anyone is in Christ, he is a new creation; old things have passed away; behold, all things have become new (2 Cor. 5:17).

Then He who sat on the throne said, "Behold, I make all things new." And He said to me, "Write, for these words are true and faithful" (Rev. 21:5).

There is much that is new when God is at work.

In the New Testament we are told that our lives do have significance. The apostle Paul talked of living all his life in the light of eternity: "I press toward the goal for the prize of the upward call of God in Christ Jesus" (Phil. 3:14). He lived under the assumption that the important things are those which are unseen: "We do not look at the things which are seen, but at the things which are not seen. For the things which are seen are temporary, but the things which are not seen are eternal" (2 Cor. 4:18).

Solomon has driven home his point: the one who does not live by belief in God hopes against hope. In that condition life can only be "vanity"—fleeting, vaporous, meaningless. Only a belief in the one true God will give anyone a basis for hope or a meaningful life.

Just as surely, since Christ is God's giving of Himself to us, those who put Him at the center of their lives transcend the hopelessness of work, nature, the senses, and history. Jesus said, "I am the way, the truth, and the life" (John 14:6).

It is still true.

CHAPTER THREE

Where Am I to Find Happiness and Satisfaction?

Ecclesiastes 1:12–2:26

All of us have restless hearts. There is something in us that is never really satisfied, never content. We want more. We want better. We want.

A friend told me of a sales job he held several years ago. Unsure of himself, he worked harder and longer than the rest of the sales staff to prove himself. Beginning with the company's poorest sales territory, he turned it into the second best before his first year was completed. From that time on, until the day he burned out and collapsed, he never had less than a 100 per cent increase in sales each year. "I would go in for my annual review each December," he said, "and my boss would look at my sales figures, grin, and say, 'I've only got one word to say. *More!*'"

Shaking his head, my friend smiled, "You know, I should have been mad. I was already doing the best job in the company. But it never bothered me, because it was the same word that haunted me every day of the year. More! I drove myself over the edge. I can't blame anyone else. I was just never satisfied with what I did, even when it was the best."

King Solomon had more. Because he was a king, he could try everything in life his heart desired. And after having searched the same places we search—intellectual pursuits, pleasure, social and material achievement—he concluded that there was no real satisfaction to be found in any of them.

So he decided to conduct an experiment.

We understand experiments. From our youth we are taught how to test ideas, see if they work, evaluate them, and draw our conclusions. Watch Solomon as he tests life to see if there is any satisfaction to be found in the places where we all look.

> I, the Preacher, was king over Israel in Jerusalem. And I set my heart to seek and search out by wisdom concerning all that is done

under heaven; this grievous task God has given to the sons of man, by which they may be exercised. I have seen all the works that are done under the sun; and indeed, all is vanity and grasping for the wind.

> What is crooked
>   cannot be made straight,
> And what is lacking
>   cannot be numbered (1:12–15).

Solomon begins his experiment by revealing his conclusion. He summarizes it and goes beyond just what may be observed in nature. He knows that all of us are restless and unsatisfied; that much can be observed. But he attributes this dissatisfaction to God: "It is an unhappy business that God has given to the sons of men to be busy with" (1:13 RSV). Interestingly enough, much later the apostle Paul made much the same point: "For the creation was subjected to futility" (Rom. 8:20).

The wisdom of which Solomon talks is human, secular wisdom. The "unhappy business" is every human activity that lacks God at the center; it is an inevitable result of living without God as the focus of one's life. It was true then. It is true now. Everything we can observe in this world is pointless in itself. It goes nowhere; it is like "grasping for the wind." Down inside we know there is more, but we cannot grasp it. Every time we think we have almost found it, it evades us.

That is what life is like.

Furthermore, we cannot change it. "What is crooked cannot be made straight, and what is lacking cannot be numbered" (1:15). Today's English Version says it well, "You can't straighten out what is crooked; you can't count things that aren't there." There are many things we cannot change. Life has many flaws; it always will.

Recently, I was driving with my family in northern Minnesota. It had been a long day, and toward evening we stopped for a pizza. As we sat there unwinding and enjoying the relaxed atmosphere, a young couple and their two small sons came in and sat next to us. I took one look at the situation and knew the peace and quiet was over. My mind flashed back to when our own children were young and we were someone else's disturbance. Now it was our turn to be on the receiving end. There will always be crooked things that cannot be made straight!

It was not long after this experience that I had a speaking engagement in another city. As I boarded the airplane to return home, I noticed that the businessman across the aisle in the row behind me had his attaché case open and had taken out his clipboard to do some paperwork. He appeared pleased with life, until a young woman with one baby in her arms and another in an infant seat, along with a two-year-old toddler, crowded into the two seats next to him. It seemed as if all three children cried or yelled throughout the entire flight. At one point I turned to see how he was doing. I will never forget the look on his face. It was as if he had received a painful, fatal injection and was waiting for it to take effect.

There will always be problems and annoyances in our lives that simply cannot be corrected. Tired, afraid, upset babies will always be with us, God bless them! So will sickness, hatred, injustice, and untimely death.

The bad news is that it will always be that way. Even the best things in life have their defects. But the good news is that they do not have to affect your inner joy. External circumstances do not make or break us; how we handle them is far more important.

THE EXPERIMENT

Solomon begins to examine the best things the observable world has to offer us. They are the things that we still seek today; and if we will look over his shoulder as he conducts his experiment, we will gain the benefit of his experience.

First, Solomon examines *wisdom.* Keep in mind, he is looking at the observable world, the world apart from God, the world "under the sun." We need to distinguish the wisdom he is evaluating—human knowledge—from true wisdom, which comes from God (see Prov. 9:10) and matures us to see things as God does (1 Cor. 2:6–16).

> I communed with my heart, saying, "Look, I have attained greatness, and have gained more wisdom than all who were before me in Jerusalem. My heart has understood great wisdom and knowledge."

And I set my heart to know wisdom and to know madness and folly.
I perceived that this also is grasping for the wind.

For in much wisdom is much grief,
And he who increases knowledge increases sorrow (1:16–18).

What did he discover? After probing wisdom "to know wisdom and to know madness and folly"—that is, so he could be wise rather than foolish—he declared "this also is grasping for the wind." Why? The more he learned, the more reason he had for grief and sorrow. The clearer he could think, the more clearly he could see how easily life can go wrong and that nothing on earth is permanent.

The more we learn, the more we realize how little we know. As we discover new information, we see whole areas where we know nothing and in which we can never hope to learn anything. We realize that we live in a world where our knowledge is limited and our ability to control the future is an illusion.

The more we learn, the clearer we see how precarious life really is. All of us die (see 2:15); eventually time and chance get to us (see 9:11–12); we never know whether once we are gone our efforts will prosper or fail (see 2:19). There are no guarantees; and the more clearly we look at life, the more vividly we see that.

The more we know, the more we see how we make mistake after mistake. Our blunders are embarrassing; they also bring us much grief.

More knowledge does not necessarily lead to more enlightened living; frequently it leads to greater evil. We live in the day of the knowledge explosion, and yet mankind is closer than ever to destroying itself with war, violence, and brutality. As one skeptic has said, "Modern technology has only served to make us more efficient in our cruelty."

We Christians need to be careful here. Further education is fine; it may be smack in the center of God's will for you. But don't ever use your pursuit of knowledge to provide the satisfaction and peace that can be found only in Christ and His kingdom. The enemy of our souls can easily take an M.A. or Ph.D. after our names and make it an idol.

So what do we do? I believe in getting a good education. We should encourage our children in school. We should continue learning as adults. But scholarly wisdom that has no room for God at its center is of no ultimate value. We must seek the wisdom that comes from God.

Second, Solomon examines *pleasure*. Why not? We can relate to pleasure! We live in a time when there are more pleasures available—good and bad—than we could ever experience. Our society is saturated with the pursuit of pleasure.

> I said in my heart, "Come now, I will test you with mirth; therefore enjoy pleasure"; but surely, this also was vanity. I said of laughter, "It is madness"; and of mirth, "What does it accomplish?" I searched in my heart how to gratify my flesh with wine, while guiding my heart with wisdom, and how to lay hold on folly, till I might see what was good for the sons of men to do under heaven all the days of their lives (2:1–3).

Who could test pleasure more thoroughly than a king? Solomon had more wealth and power than anyone, so why not? If wisdom will not give us what we expect from it, let's escape into hedonism. Solomon's conclusion? "This also was vanity" (2:1).

In another place Solomon wrote, "A merry heart does good, like medicine" (Prov. 17:22). So he is not making light of the value of entertainment or laughter, only of expecting more from it than it can provide. Laughter can be therapeutic. We need it. But when it is what we live for, when it is a goal of our lives rather than a result, it eludes us.

So why not get drunk? "I searched my heart how to gratify my flesh with wine" (v. 3). Surely he knew better. He himself had painted a vivid picture of the alcohol-saturated life.

> Who has woe?
> Who has sorrow?
> Who has contentions?
> Who has complaints?
> Who has wounds without cause?
> Who has redness of eyes?
> Those who linger long at the wine,
> Those who go in search of mixed wine.
> Do not look on the wine when it is red,
> When it sparkles in the cup,

When it swirls around smoothly;
At the last it bites like a serpent,
And stings like a viper.
Your eyes will see strange things,
And your heart will utter perverse things,
Yes, you will be like one who lies down in the midst of the sea,
Or like one who lies at the top of the mast, saying:
'They have struck me, but I was not hurt;
They have beaten me, but I did not feel it.
When shall I awake, that I may seek another drink?' (Prov. 23:29–
35).

With the large numbers of automobile accidents, divorce, and child abuse cases related to drinking, it is obvious that people continue to seek pleasure through drunkenness. And it is no less vain and empty today than it was in Solomon's time.

Note that Solomon does not say it is wrong to enjoy ourselves. We need pleasure, just as we need knowledge. But the apostle Paul's advice holds true: "Therefore, whether you eat or drink, or whatever you do, do all to the glory of God" (1 Cor. 10:31). We are to live for God's glory. When we do so, all of life will be sacred, including our pleasure. But pleasure will not bring us the satisfaction we desire.

Third, Solomon examines *achievement*. He has covered the bases now. If you find someone who is not immersed in education or pleasure, chances are he or she is striving for success. Millions look for their satisfaction here, especially if they have tried the others and found them wanting. Could so many people be wrong? Listen to Solomon's words:

I made my works great, I built myself houses, and planted myself vineyards. I made myself gardens and orchards, and I planted all kinds of fruit trees in them. I made myself waterpools from which to water the growing trees of the grove. I acquired male and female servants, and had servants born in my house. Yes, I had greater possessions of herds and flocks than all who were in Jerusalem before me. I also gathered for myself silver and gold and the special treasures of kings and of the provinces. I acquired male and female singers, the delights of the sons of men, and musical instruments of all kinds. So I became great and excelled more than all who were before me in Jerusalem. Also my wisdom remained with me.

Whatever my eyes desired I did not keep from them.
I did not withhold my heart from any pleasure,
For my heart rejoiced in all my labor;
And this was my reward from all my labor.
Then I looked on all the works that my hands had done
And on the labor in which I had toiled;
And indeed all was vanity and grasping for the wind.
There was no profit under the sun (2:4–11).

Solomon tried to create his own Garden of Eden. He built houses and vineyards and parks and orchards. He made pools and bought slaves and herds and flocks. He accumulated silver and gold, musicians and concubines. He indulged every whim and satisfied every appetite imaginable. Very few persons could match his ability to give the acid test to achievement. If anyone could find satisfaction in his accomplishments, certainly King Solomon would have done so. Even our modern millionaires, with all their wealth, could not outdo him.

He even enjoyed his job! But what was Solomon's verdict?

Then I looked on all the works that my hands had done
And on the labor in which I had toiled;
And indeed all was vanity and grasping for the wind.
There was no profit under the sun" (2:11).

"It's not here either! I still haven't found anything worthwhile. It's all vanity, empty. Achievement is empty. Possessions are like grasping at the wind. Nothing can be gained from them."

How good of God to share this experiment with us! We can learn from it and not make the same mistakes.

But we can learn from our pasts, too. Remember that object you just *had* to have. You positively knew it would bring satisfaction. Did it? Of course not.

SOLOMON'S EVALUATION OF HUMAN DESIRE

So far Solomon has been very harsh on the things that people desire the most—knowledge, pleasure, achievement. He now doubles back over his experiment to evaluate and explain just why it turned out as it did. He begins with wisdom and pleasure, or folly.

Then I turned myself to consider wisdom and madness and folly;
For what can the man do who succeeds the king?—
Only what he has already done.
Then I saw that wisdom excels folly
As light excels darkness.
The wise man's eyes are in his head,
But the fool walks in darkness.
Yet I myself perceived
That the same event happens to them all.
So I said in my heart,
"As it happens to the fool,
It also happens to me,
And why was I then more wise?"
Then I said in my heart, "This also is vanity."
For there is no more remembrance of the wise than of the fool
    forever,
Since all that now is will be forgotten in the days to come.
And how does a wise man die?
As the fool!

Therefore I hated life because the work that was done under the sun was grievous to me, for all is vanity and grasping for the wind (2:12–17).

Solomon had been testing wisdom and folly in his experiment. He recognized that we might be tempted to doubt the truth of his experiment; so he reminds us, "For what can the man do who succeeds the king?" It is as if he is saying, "Come on, now. I'm a hard act to follow. What are you going to try that I haven't done? In fact, you can only do *some* of what I've done."

Even wisdom without God is better than foolishness without Him. It is as much better as light is to darkness (see 2:13). A wise man has his eyes "in his head," but a fool walks around as though his eyes are shut (see 2:14).

And yet, there is a problem. It is a simple one: we are human beings, and we will die. If "the same event happens to them all . . ." (2:14), ". . . why was I then more wise?" (2:15). If the wise man and the fool suffer the same fate, why seek wisdom? To add insult to injury, Solomon reminds us that both the fool and the wise man "will be forgotten in the days to come." No one will even remember them.

What is more mortifying about our mortality than this! It mocks everything important to us.

There is a solution. In chapter 3, verse 11, Solomon gives his answer. What we see here is not the whole picture. If we eliminate God from our lives, the gloomy view is the right one. But when we live for God, life takes on new meaning.

There is a godly wisdom that makes all the difference in the world. The Book of Daniel speaks of it: "Those who are wise shall shine/Like the brightness of the firmament,/And those who turn many to righteousness/Like the stars forever and ever" (12:3). And in Revelation 14:13 we are told, concerning those who die in the Lord, "Blessed are the dead who die in the Lord from now on. 'Yes,' says the Spirit, 'that they may rest from their labors, and their works follow them.'"

The fact that Solomon was bitter about this cruel hoax—"Therefore I hated life" (2:17)—also says something about the solution to the dilemma it poses. It almost reaches forward to the marvelous words of chapter 3, "Also He has put eternity in their hearts" (v. 11), to declare Solomon's faith and explain where satisfaction can be found.

Solomon is not ready to quit his experiment. He wants to keep at it. So he returns to man's achievements. But even there, only bitterness is to be found.

Then I hated all my labor in which I had toiled under the sun, because I must leave it to the man who will come after me. And who knows whether he will be a wise man or a fool? Yet he will rule over all my labor in which I toiled and in which I have shown myself wise under the sun. This also is vanity. Therefore I turned my heart and despaired of all the labor in which I had toiled under the sun. For there is a man whose labor is with wisdom, knowledge, and skill; yet he must leave his heritage to a man who has not labored for it. This also is vanity and a great evil. For what has man for all his labor, and for the striving of his heart with which he has toiled under the sun? For all his days are sorrowful, and his work grievous; even in the night his heart takes no rest. This also is vanity (2:18–23).

Remember now, he was the king. It is not as if he were under-employed. Being king is not a bad job! But he is angry—*mad!* "It really angers me," he is saying. "I'm going to work hard all my life. I'm going to amass a fortune, and someone else will get it. I don't like that at all." And furthermore, "He might be a fool and waste it." In fact, that is exactly what Solomon's son Rehoboam did. He played the fool and took poor advice, and his kingdom was split (see 1 Kin. 12).

There is an interesting lesson to be found here. Solomon talks about the man whose consuming passion is his work; he has so much on his mind that he cannot sleep at night (see 2:23). The psalmist wrote, "It is vain for you to rise up early,/To sit up late,/To eat the bread of sorrows;/For so He gives His beloved sleep" (Ps. 127:2). God wants us to work, but He wants us to order our priorities and not make an idol of our work.

Jesus had the best plan when He said, "Come to Me, all you who labor and are heavy laden, and I will give you rest" (Matt. 11:28). He did not mean that we would no longer need to work and could lie around all day. He will give us rest *in* our work. "Take My yoke upon you . . . and you will find rest for your souls. For My yoke is easy and My burden is light" (Matt. 11:29–30). It is still a yoke; but it is the yoke of Jesus, and it fits. It does not chafe. It is good, for there is rest in our souls in the midst of our labor.

I have often thought of how Jesus lived His life. As far as I can tell, He was never in a hurry and He never wasted time. When I am in a hurry, I am going faster than He is. When I am wasting time— and I am not talking about relaxation or entertainment—I am a poor steward. Jesus never gives us more to do than He gives us time to do it.

SATISFACTION

What is Solomon's conclusion to the matter? He repeats this message in 9:7–10 and in 11:7–10, but his basic point is that satisfaction comes in receiving God's gifts and using them for the purpose He intends.

> There is nothing better for a man than that he should eat and drink, and that his soul should enjoy good in his labor. This also, I saw, was from the hand of God. For who can eat, or who can have enjoyment more than I? For God gives wisdom and knowledge and joy to a man

who is good in His sight; but to the sinner He gives the work of gathering and collecting, that he may give to him who is good before God. This also is vanity and grasping for the wind (2:24–26).

Verse 24 can be translated from Hebrew to English as, "There is nothing inherent in man that allows him to enjoy eating and drinking and finding enjoyment in his toil." Let me say it another way: "Man has nothing within himself that allows him to enjoy life." We cannot enjoy life apart from God.

That is the sum of the matter.

The experiment is a failure, as far as secular man is concerned. What began as a grand program to discover all those wonderful areas of life where we can be the masters of our fates and the captains of our souls has been reduced to the simple fact that man does not have the ability to find satisfaction in anything!

Satisfaction is a gift from God, just like salvation. When we can take our knowledge, our pleasure, and our work as gifts from God, then our search has found its goal. And all the good things God has in store for us are ours.

Death will take away none of that satisfaction.

There is a crowning irony in the last verse of this chapter. Notice the contrast between what God gives—wisdom, knowledge, and joy—and what mankind strives so hard to amass but cannot keep. Even that, we are told, will go to the righteous. But the righteous have their treasure in heaven (see Matt. 6:21). Their hearts will be there, too.

CHAPTER FOUR

How Can I Fit into God's Plans?

Ecclesiastes 3:1–15

In his book, *Born Again,* Charles Colson told of his conversion to Christ following the reelection of President Nixon and the accompanying scandals that shocked the world.

The book opened with a revealing election-night scene that preceded Colson's troubles with the Watergate prosecutors. Standing in the elegant Washington, D.C., hotel, he realized that they had managed an unprecedented landslide victory. At the same time, he was puzzled over the uneasiness that was gnawing at him even in his moment of triumph.

Later that night, after several hours alone with the president of the United States, he realized that something was seriously wrong. A deadness was eating away at him; even the most exhilarating of human achievements could not hide it.

There is something in each of us that says there has to be more to life than what we see and experience. So much of what we do seems meaningless over the long run. We mow the grass; it grows and we have to mow it again. We clean the house; it gets dirty and we have to clean it again. We go to work, pick up a pay check, and spend it; we go back to work so we can pick up another pay check and spend it. We cook all day, or so it seems, to eat our meals; the next day we do it all over again.

If you are like me, every once in a while you look at all this activity and say, "What is the point of it all? Why am I doing this?" Surely, life has to be more than mowing grass, cleaning house, working, cooking, eating. We want to give our lives to more than this; we want them to be meaningful.

Solomon understood that feeling. He undoubtedly experienced it himself. And he knew that the secular-minded person feels it, too. So, as a part of his ongoing apologetic for the spiritual life, he painted another vivid word picture. In this picture he declares that

God's plan encompasses everything, even mowing lawns and cleaning house and changing diapers and earning a living. All of it.

GOD'S ALL-ENCOMPASSING PLAN

> To everything there is a season,
>   A time for every purpose under heaven (3:1).

At first glance it is reassuring to know that "there is a right time for everything," as *The Living Bible* reads. To illustrate his statement, Solomon then proceeds to list fourteen pairs of opposites that are a part of God's plan that man must acknowledge.

> A time to be born,
>   And a time to die;
> A time to plant,
>   And a time to pluck
>   what is planted;
> A time to kill,
>   And a time to heal;
> A time to break down,
>   And a time to build up;
> A time to weep,
>   And a time to laugh;
> A time to mourn,
>   And a time to dance;
> A time to cast away stones,
>   And a time to gather stones;
> A time to embrace,
>   And a time to refrain from
>   embracing;
> A time to gain,
>   And a time to lose;
> A time to keep,
>   And a time to throw away;
> A time to tear,
>   And a time to sew;
> A time to keep silence,
>   And a time to speak;
> A time to love,
>   And a time to hate;

> A time of war,
> And a time of peace (3:2–8).

This list must have driven Solomon's secular adversary wild! While there is something very comforting about the rhythmic regularity he reports, this regularity has some disturbing implications. First, if everything is part of God's plan and has its time, then I must not be as free as I thought. Someone or something bigger than I must be calling the shots or making the rules. After all, I have very little choice about the circumstances that cause me to weep or to laugh.

Second, and equally devastating, this list implies that nothing I do has permanence. "If I'm only going to die, why be born? And if what I build up will only break down, why bother doing anything?" While the believer (who knows who is in charge) finds great comfort in this regularity, it is a devastating problem for the person who leaves God out of the picture.

Solomon knew this, and his adversary knew it. So do the purveyors of our popular culture who lament the hopelessness they experience without God while they continue their dance of death, stubbornly refusing to acknowledge Him in any meaningful way.

For a moment let us look at the end of the book where Solomon gives us the key to his logic. How can he look at this endless cycle and see freedom and meaning where the secular man can only see slavery and meaninglessness? The basis for Solomon's security lies in these words:

> Let us hear the conclusion of the whole matter: Fear God and keep His commandments, for this is the whole duty of man. For God will bring every work into judgment, including every secret thing, whether it is good or whether it is evil (12:13–14).

That is the key: God is in charge. The one who fears God, or honors Him, and keeps His commandments can be secure in the gracious love of the One who created him. That is where the difference lies.

It is interesting to observe the contrasts in these verses. God's plan includes our birth and our death (see v. 2), both of which are beyond our control, as well as the growing and harvesting of crops. It includes killing—perhaps a reference to war or executing those who have taken the life of one made in God's image (see Gen. 9:6)—and healing, as well as times when families and nations are divided and times when they are strengthened (see v. 3). (See Jeremiah 18:7–9 for an interesting example of this.)

God's plan includes times for sorrow and for joy, times for mourning and for celebration (see v. 4). This is an interesting example of Hebrew poetry, for the two lines of this verse are precisely parallel. The poetry is in the idea instead of in the sound of the words, as in a rhyme.

The first half of verse five has puzzled interpreters. Many have assumed that it is meant literally: there is a time to throw stones (as in rocks) and a time to pick them up for building walls and buildings. Others suggest that the "time to cast away stones" refers to incidents like those that appear in 2 Kings 3:19, 25, where God commanded the Israelites to tear down the cities of the Moabites and make their fields unuseable by littering them with the stones.

Jewish rabbis, however, have long taught a more likely interpretation, for they see the word "stones" as a euphemism for male testes and therefore find the first half of the verse saying that there is a time to have intercourse ("cast away stones")—for instance, when one's wife is "clean" according to the Law—and there is a time to refrain from intercourse ("gather stones")—for instance, when one's wife is menstrually "unclean." (See Leviticus 12:2; 15:24; 18:19; 20:18 for specific mention of this in the Law.)

If this interpretation is correct, then the second half of the verse, which refers to embracing and refraining from embracing, would be parallel with the first half.

I believe this is what Solomon was saying: "There are appropriate and inappropriate times for sexual love." While Christians today are no longer bound to the Old Testament laws of ritual purity, we would do well to remember that the laws of moral purity are clearly reaffirmed by the writers of the New Testament and by Jesus Himself. Indeed, Jesus made a point of calling His followers to a very high view of sex; sex is reserved exclusively for our mate, and our thoughts are to be as pure as our actions are to be upright (Matt. 5:27–32).

God's plan includes gain and loss (see v. 6), an interesting comment in view of Solomon's statement in 1:3 that there is no profit, no gain. Similarly, there is a time to guard what we have and a time to give away our possessions. God's plan includes mourning and ceasing one's mourning (see v. 7); the reference to tearing one's clothes probably refers to the custom of tearing one's garments as an expression of grief and mending them when the time of mourning was complete (see 2 Samuel 13:31 for an example of this custom).

There are times when it is best to speak, and other times when it is prudent to remain silent, or when it is a waste of one's efforts to speak (see v. 7).

Even the calamities of life are in God's plan. The love and hate mentioned in verse 8 do not refer to personal relationships so much as to affairs among the nations. There is also "a time of war" when God takes up the sword to destroy the wicked nations of the earth, and a time in His plan when peace is to rule.

Several years ago a popular song, "Turn, Turn, Turn," used these verses for its lyrics. As the secular world usually does, it turned the meaning of this passage on its head. Wedding its beautiful and haunting melody to these words, it lamented, "I hope we're not too late" (to stop the war).

I use this illustration to show how devastating to secular man is the idea that in God's plan there is a time for *everything.* I dislike war as much as anyone; I hate it. I believe God does, too, even when He has to use it to bring judgment among the nations. But even our greatest plans fail (see v. 6). People die and wars erupt, and only the person who trusts in the goodness of God can look it all in the face and know that somehow it is contained in the providence of God. This is not to say that the Lord plans our troubles, but He permits them. He makes everything work together with all life's experiences for good.

People with a temporal value system have trouble understanding God's providence. It is as difficult for the secular mind today as it was in Solomon's time; but, nevertheless, it is still true. God can be trusted to accomplish His own purposes!

GOD MAKES EVEN THE UNLOVELY BEAUTIFUL

At best, we see only a small part of what is happening in God's world. God's plan is not chaos; it is purposeful change. It has a beginning and an end. Everything fits together.

What profit has the worker from that in which he labors? I have seen
the God-given task with which the sons of men are to be occupied.
He has made everything beautiful in its time (3:9–11).

Again we return to the theme of Ecclesiastes 1:3: "What profit
has a man from all his labor in which he toils under the sun?" After
all the seasons are over, what is my profit? What have I gained?
And, as Solomon has done repeatedly, he forces the secularist to
confront all those opposites that neutralize each other. "If I'm here
and then die, it would make just as much sense if I hadn't been
born at all, wouldn't it?" (This may, in fact, be the basis on which
the secular mind justifies abortion: What difference does it make?)
"If there is a time for sewing and a time for tearing, why bother
sewing? What profit, what point is there in doing anything?"

Having exposed the moral bankruptcy of a secular viewpoint,
Solomon presses home the point he wishes to make. "I've seen these
opposites. I know they are real. But God has ordained them, and
'He has made everything beautiful in its time.'"

The word *beautiful* had a wider meaning than aesthetic beauty; it
also means "appropriate." God has made everything appropriate for
its time; it all fits. So when each part of our lives "fits" God's plan, it
is beautiful, appropriate. Romans 8:28 says the same thing: "And
we know that all things work together for good to those who love
God, to those who are called according to His purpose."

Neither Solomon nor the apostle Paul say that we will like
everything in life. We might even become the victims of murder,
war, or business failure. That is in God's hands. But—happy days
or sad, good circumstances or evil—when all our life is within
God's plan, it is appropriate and beautiful for the person who fears
God and keeps His commandments (see 12:13).

Let me illustrate this. If you go to the Minnesota State Fair, you
will notice that some of the heavy-equipment companies bring a
very unusual object along with their displays. They bring a model
of an engine with part of it cut away so you can see the gears at
work. Some gears go in one direction, and others go another; but
they all work together to make the axle go in the direction the
person operating the vehicle chooses.

When looking at the gears in a machine, people often wonder,
"How can one gear go this way, one another, and others go theirs,

and yet the axle turns the wheel the right direction?" Someone designed it to work that way.

Life works like that engine. Some things go our way, and some things appear to go against us. Actually, who are we to know which is which? We experience all sorts of events, and for the life of us we cannot tell how it is working together for good. But it is. It is beautiful. It is appropriate.

God made it that way.

Being born and dying. Weeping and laughing. Sewing and tearing. Planting and reaping. Killing and healing. War and peace. God is big enough to handle all of it.

GOD'S PLAN REQUIRES US TO RETURN TO HIM

Several years ago a man sailed from the United States to England in a one-person rowboat. In the celebration that followed his arrival, a reporter asked his wife if she had been afraid he would fail. "Oh, no," she replied. "I know the one who made the boat."

It is important to know the One who made the plan. It is important to know what He is like.

> Also He has put eternity in their hearts, except that no one can find out the work that God does from beginning to end (3:11).

Solomon says God has put eternity in our hearts. What is that "eternity"? It is that part of you that says, "I am made for more than all this. Yes. I sow and reap and clean and cook and eat. But the clothes are going to wear out, and I will have to harvest the grain again next year, and the house will get dirty, and I will have to prepare my meals again tomorrow. But I do not live for that!"

God has put within us the knowledge that this world is not enough. He created us to have intellectual curiosity, but he did not give us the capacity to know everything about life. We cannot know how all of life fits together. "No one can find out the work that God does from beginning to end" (3:11). How wonderful! Frequently someone says to me, "I don't know how that fits into God's plan for my life." And I say, "I don't either, but God does." That should be enough for all of us. If we knew all that God knows, what kind of God would we have?

We are very much like the desperately near-sighted person who has to inch himself along a great mural. He sees enough to know it is a great work of art, but he cannot step back to see how it fits together. He sees some of this and some of that, but he cannot see all of it. We are like that. We inch along through life like a near-sighted art connoisseur. We see some bright colors and say, "Oh, how lovely. Isn't God good?" Then we see some dark, ominous clouds and we say, "How could that be part of a beautiful work of art?" Those who live in relationship with God know the One who painted the mural. We realize that the great work of art that God is making in our lives requires the dark and ominous colors along with the bright ones.

We are to rejoice and enjoy life; it is God's gift to us. The times of weeping and the times of rejoicing both come from God. We can trust the Painter. We "know the One who made the boat."

IT'S ALL FOREVER

The truth expressed in verses 12–15 contain very different meanings for the believer and the unbeliever.

> I know that there is nothing better for them than to rejoice, and to do good in their lives, and also that every man should eat and drink and enjoy the good of all his labor—it is the gift of God.

> I know that whatever God does,
> It shall be forever.
> Nothing can be added to it,
> And nothing taken from it.
> God does it, that men should fear before Him.
> That which is has already been,
> And what is to be has already been;
> And God requires an account of what is past (3:12–15).

For the unbeliever, these words signify utter hopelessness. Since everything is God's gift (see v. 13) and we cannot add to or subtract from God's work (see v. 14), the unbeliever is trapped in a system that cannot bend or break.

To the modern secular mind, verses 14 and 15 are a cry of despair. There is no hope, no exit (to borrow a phrase from the

French existentialist philosopher, Jean-Paul Sartre). Existence is a closed system for the unbeliever; he cannot escape it or make it bend or break. Therefore, this message becomes a severe burden. "Therefore consider the goodness and severity of God: on those who fell, severity; but toward you, goodness, if you continue in His goodness" (Rom. 11:22).

But it is a far different story for the one who knows God. If God is love (see 1 John 4:8), then nothing is in vain (in contrast to man's efforts, 1:3); for His love lasts forever. The times of weeping and of laughter both come from Him. His plans need no mid-course corrections (see 3:14).

Earlier, in describing the world as secular man experiences it, Solomon said, "Life is so vain. It does not last; it is transitory." But now, speaking of the truth and not describing the predicament of the man who ignores God, he says, "As a matter of fact, life is not temporary. What God does lasts forever." It is only because of our limited vision that the events of life seem so disjointed.

Why is life like that? "God does it, that men should fear before Him" (3:14). In several other verses in Ecclesiastes, Solomon says we are to fear God (see 5:7; 7:18; 8:12–13 [3 times]; 12:13). Why is it so important for us to fear the Lord?

First, remember the commandment, "You shall have no other gods before Me" (Ex. 20:3). God alone is God. He alone knows everything. If we knew what He knows, then we would be as God (see Is. 14:14). Indeed, we would be God.

But even more important, the fear of God represents a relationship of love. In thanking God for His provision of forgiveness, the psalmist says, "But there is forgiveness with You, that You may be feared" (Ps. 130:4). The fear of God is a response of love for His goodness in creating us and in forgiving us of our sin. To fear God is to love Him, to commit ourselves to Him without reservation, and to say, "Lord, you alone are Lord. And I love you."

We do not always see that everything is beautiful, or appropriate. But we can believe it because of what we know about God. Knowing His character, and knowing Him personally, gives us the basis for the faith that "He has made everything beautiful in its time."

CHAPTER FIVE

The Harsh Realities of Life

Ecclesiastes 3:16–4:3; 5:8–9; 7:7

There is much in this world that brings us joy: the many pleasures of life—rewarding work, loving relationships, quiet rest.

But there is also another side to the world—the dark side. Mourning and weeping are as real as singing and laughing. Anger and war are as real as love and peace. Throughout the tapestry of life there runs a dark, harsh thread that cannot be ignored. Even on our best days, the harsh realities of life affect us.

Earlier in chapter three Solomon reminded us of the fact that we cannot understand everything about life. "He has made everything beautiful in its time. Also He has put eternity in their hearts, except that no one can find out the work that God does from beginning to end" (3:11).

Life is beautiful, we are told. It is appropriate; it fits. On the other hand, none of us can see the beginning or the end to see how it fits. We know it does, by faith; but we do not know how. We are, as it were, mentally nearsighted.

We need to see these realities as God sees them. We need to see how God makes use of them so that by faith they are beautiful to us. This way of seeing is not natural for us. We are hurt by the dark side of life, as we see the unbelievable tragedies around us. Yet, by faith we trust that God has a plan.

INJUSTICE

We regularly read of injustices in magazines and newspapers; radio and television report the latest injustices with alarming frequency. Solomon saw injustice, too.

Moreover I saw under the sun:
In the place of judgment,

Wickedness was there;
And in the place of righteousness,
Iniquity was there.
I said in my heart,
"God shall judge the righteous and the wicked,
For there shall be a time there for every purpose and for every
    work" (3:16–17).

These words remind us of verses 2–8, where everything is subject to reversal. Here, however, injustice, of all things, becomes an
exception! Ironically, injustice is one reality we wish *would* be
reversed. "At least here," we might say, "we can find some gain!"
(See 1:3.)

God provided for human courts and tribunals to execute justice.
They are part of His plan for bringing justice into a sinful world;
their corruption illustrates how profoundly we need them. Our
frustration lies in the fact that our days, as well as our sight, are
limited; we cannot "find out the work that God does from beginning to end" (3:11). We cannot see the consequences of injustice in
the immediate future.

Secular man has been getting by with injustice for thousands of
years; he believes that God's justice will never prevail, if he even
bothers to consider the subject. But God says, "Listen, a day is
coming when man's day will end and my day will begin."

The wicked plots against the just,
And gnashes at him with his teeth.
The Lord laughs at him,
For He sees that his day is coming (Ps. 37:12–13).

The believer knows better than to despair. He knows that ultimately God will judge every person's work. "He has appointed a
day on which He will judge the world in righteousness by the Man
whom He has ordained" (Acts 17:31). The day has already been
determined; God has declared this by raising Jesus from the dead.

DECEPTIVE PROSPERITY

While attending college, I patronized a service station run by
two partners, John and Andy. John was a dishonest, ungodly sort of

fellow. Andy was a committed Christian, and it was a delight to do business with him. One would think that Andy would have prospered; everyone preferred doing business with him. And, after all, don't we reap what we sow?

A few years after graduation I returned to the filling station, only to find that John had bought out Andy's interest in the business. John went on to be fairly successful in business, while Andy never enjoyed strong financial success. How can that be?

Psalm 73 deals with this question quite pointedly, declaring that the ungodly have a way of creating the circumstances for their own downfall, whether as a consequence of their own greed or by God's direct intervention.

> "When I thought how to understand this,
> It was too painful for me—
> Until I went into the sanctuary of God;
> Then I understood their end.
> Surely You set them in slippery places;
> You cast them down to destruction.
> Oh, how they are brought to desolation, as in a moment!
> They are utterly consumed with terrors.
> As a dream when one awakes,
> So, Lord, when You awake,
> You shall despise their image" (Ps. 73:16–20).

Every man, woman, and child is accountable to God. When God comes to pass judgment and bring relief to this world, justice will prevail. The results are not in yet. We can see it now by faith, even if it is not manifest in our midst. That is how Solomon faced the reality of injustice; so must we. We need to see it from God's perspective.

Solomon's advice is fine for the believer; it provides comfort, even if it does not offer immediate relief. But it cannot be much help for the secularist. If he cares anything about justice, his solution is to tinker with the machinery (reform) or throw it away and start over (revolution). Secular man never considers the possibility that someday God will transform the world, and he certainly cannot accept his own sinful nature. So when he is told that every human effort to achieve justice will ultimately fail, he is once again brought to the end of his rope.

Man will not create a great society, or even a good one. Injustice will exist as long as sin exists. And all of us who work for justice on earth—*and we should*—must realize that Utopia will not come as a result of even our best efforts. Perfect peace and justice will only exist when Christ returns to establish His kingdom, the kingdom of God. Our efforts will only create relative peace and justice, at best.

DEATH

Death is the ultimate harsh reality. It represents finality for the person whose sole orientation is to this life; it suggests pain and sorrow even for the believer. In picking up this subject, Solomon declares that even death is "beautiful in its time." It is part of God's provision.

> I said in my heart, "Concerning the estate of the sons of men, God tests them, that they may see that they themselves are like beasts." For what happens to the sons of men also happens to beasts; one thing befalls them: as one dies, so dies the other. Surely, they all have one breath; man has no advantage over beasts, for all is vanity. All go to one place: all are from the dust, and all return to dust" (3:18–20).

Death forces us to remember that we are creatures, not the Creator. If we are like the beasts in our greed and in our mortality, then it would be wise for us to know it (see 3:18). Left to our own devices, we are likely to ignore our sinful nature. Therefore, God is merciful to remind us who we are.

Solomon is not dealing here with our eternal state (heaven or hell) once we die. And his point is not so much that we die as it is that it is the prideful man who dies. "God tests them, that they may see that they themselves are like beasts" (3:18). Our flesh is no better than the flesh of animals (see Gen. 3:19). So why should we be proud?

If we are going to limit our belief about our nature to what we can observe—and that is what Solomon is asking his secular-minded friend to do—then we are, in fact, forced to conclude that we are no better than the beasts. They die; we die. Their bodies decay; our bodies decay. They become one thing—dust (see Gen. 3:19). So do we.

Period.

For all we can see, that is the end of the matter. Or is it?

> Who knows the spirit of the sons of men, which goes upward, and the spirit of the beast, which goes down to the earth? So I perceived that there is nothing better than that a man should rejoice in his own works, for that is his heritage. For who can bring him to see what will happen after him? (3:21–22).

There is debate about how verse 21 should be translated. Whether one translates it as the New King James Version does (following the tradition of the KJV) or with the interrogative, "Who knows whether . . . ?," Solomon is clearly challenging the reader to look at what he sees every day, and nothing else, and tell him if he can observe anything different in the death of a human being and the death of an animal. Solomon knows there is a difference. He has just reminded us that we are going to die, just like the beasts. He knows that for the beast it is the end of everything, but not so for man. We cannot prove it from anything we can see. So, "Who knows . . . ?" That is exactly the point.

Solomon knows, and so do we. He knows that the spirit of man does not cease to exist at death. Yes, the body does deteriorate, just as the body of an animal decomposes; but the spirit goes to God, either for punishment or reward. Some will enjoy God's "Enter into the joy of your master" (Matt. 25:21). Others will hear, "I never knew you; depart from Me" (Matt. 7:23). "Dust to dust" is not the complete story.

Death should be a comfort to the Christian. None of us desires to die, unless we are in a mental condition that has obliterated our ability to think rationally. Every Christian should be able to look at the inevitability of death and say, "I love life, but death is going to be even better than life!" That is what the apostle Paul said: "I am hard pressed between the two, having a desire to depart and be with Christ, which is far better" (Phil. 1:23) and [I pray] that you may know what is the hope of His calling . . . the riches of the glory of His inheritance in the saints" (Eph. 1:18).

The most we can say is that death mars life. We can be frustrated that we will have to leave the people and things we love, and we miss those who have died already. But we can also rejoice that the best is yet to come and that death is just the door through which we must pass to completely enter into the joy of the Lord.

That is why a believer can be joyful in the face of death.

God wants us to enjoy our lives. That is why we are told, "there is nothing better than that a man should rejoice in his own works" (3:22). The message of chapter two, verses 24 through 26, is repeated here: "The person who doesn't know the Lord cannot even enjoy this life!"—even though that is all he has! That much should be obvious. The person who believes this life is everything cannot be expected to find fulfillment in the face of death; it brings everything to nothing.

But God's plan is for us to enjoy our lives; what else are we to do with a gift? Do we give gifts to make others miserable? Hardly. Neither does God. None of us knows what tomorrow will bring, much less the next generation. Jesus told us the same thing: "Therefore do not worry about tomorrow, for tomorrow will worry about its own things" (Matt. 6:34).

For the Christian, even death is a gracious gift from the loving Lord. Through it we enter into the joy of His presence. Completely. Forever.

OPPRESSION

Oppression is a fact of life "under the sun." We would have to have our heads in the sand to miss it. Politically, we see it in the systematic violence of governments against their people. From the brutal tactics of the Communist block to the shrill, frantic anti-communism of the oppressors in rightist regimes, one reality remains consistent—oppression is a way of life in much of the world. "For the dark places of the earth are full of the habitations of cruelty" (Ps. 74:20).

> Surely oppression destroys a wise man's reason,
> And a bribe debases his heart (7:7).

The person who oppresses others, or the one who accepts a bribe, is taking the first step along the path to ignominy. Oppression and bribery twist even a wise man's mind. Oppression destroys that which makes him wise in the first place and changes his heart so that he is accessible to bribes or vulnerable to flattery (which is the bribing of one's mind). It would be better to listen to the rebukes of friends than to be corrupted by dishonest praise.

On a personal level, we see the oppression of fathers and husbands who mistake responsibility for dictatorship, the abuse of children by cruel adults, and the exploitation of workers by their employers. There is plenty of this kind of misery in our world. Solomon talked about its influence in his world, too.

Then I returned and considered all the oppression that is done under the sun:

And look! The tears of the oppressed,
But they have no comforter—
On the side of their oppressors there was power,
But they have no comforter.
Therefore I praised the dead who were already dead,
More than the living who are still alive.
Yet, better than both is he who has never existed,
Who has not seen the evil work that is done under the sun (4:1–3).

If you see the oppression of the poor, and the violent perversion of justice and righteousness in a province, do not marvel at the matter; for high official watches over high official, and higher officials are over them. Moreover the profit of the land is for all; the king himself is served from the field (5:8–9).

Solomon does not dwell on this theme at length in Ecclesiastes. Perhaps that fact alone is mute testimony to the futility (the vanity) of striving for a world free from oppression. There is little to say beyond observing the obvious fact: "on the side of their oppressors there was power" (4:1). There always is. There is something about power that breeds the habit of oppression. It frequently corrupts those who possess it.

That may be the reason Solomon does not dwell on the benefits of revolution or reform. Tyranny seems to expand to fill the power available, and the level of oppression does not seem to subside as one regime replaces another. At the same time, however, one must admit that the level of oppression varies drastically from one nation to another. What might be viewed as oppression by many in the United States would be dearly welcomed relief in Cambodia.

Solomon paints with a wide brush when he declares that "they have no comforter" (4:1). He seems to be saying that no matter what we do to comfort the oppressed or work on their behalf, oppression will still exist. Oppressors soon become comfortable with their station in life.

In chapter five, verses 8 and 9 offer an interesting explanation of how oppression is able to maintain itself. Solomon describes how oppressors justify their actions. They are able to do it by convincing themselves it is their duty, that they are just doing their job, as Adolph Eichmann described his role in sending hundreds of thousands of Jews to the gas chamber during World War II. Each official is preoccupied with his own little kingdom and turns a deaf ear to the suffering that takes place around him. In view of this same verb's use in 1 Samuel 19:11, it is likely that "watches over" implies a more predatory action than we might assume at first glance. Even the officials are oppressed by those who lord it over them.

We should "not marvel at the matter" (5:8). No utopia is around the corner. Solomon knew it, and so do we! Anyone who lives in the world of business or politics knows that power is only power when there is no doubt that those who possess it are able to use it.

When I first read verses 2 and 3 of chapter 4, I was taken back by their hopelessness.

> Therefore I praised the dead who were already dead,
> More than the living who are still alive.
> Yet, better than both is he who has never existed,
> Who has not seen the evil work that is done under the sun.

Granted, I thought, oppression is terrible; but how could anyone really believe that those who were never born are the fortunate ones?

I now believe that Solomon was speaking of evil in its most systematic and cruel forms. We do not experience that sort of oppression in our country, so perhaps we are unqualified to understand how awful oppression is. On the other hand, it is possible that Solomon is employing hyperbole (a deliberate exaggeration for its literary effect) to shock us into facing the hideous evils we find it so easy to ignore.

The secular world has no answer to this unpleasant reality of life, this "vanity of vanities." Its appeals to reform or revolution end in disillusionment all too often.

God had an answer to oppression—His Son, Jesus.

Jesus experienced the brutal realities of life. His trial was a mockery of justice, and His death was as real as any death has ever been. He was oppressed.

> He was oppressed and He was afflicted,
> Yet He opened not His mouth;
> He was led as a lamb to the slaughter,
> And as a sheep before its shearers is silent,
> So He opened not his mouth.
> He was taken from prison and from judgment,
> And who will declare His generation?
> For He was cut off from the land of the living;
> For the transgressions of My people He was stricken (Is. 53:7–8).

Jesus knew where His life was headed. He would die; He would live. And all injustice and oppression, and even death itself, would be defeated.

We are told to work at being peacemakers (Matt. 5:9). We are to feed the hungry, help the poor, visit widows and orphans, and perform many other acts of mercy and peacemaking. They all come with our calling as Christians. On one hand we work at correcting injustice and oppression, and on the other hand we realize that these evils will continue until God intervenes in history to establish His kingdom.

In the meantime, we live in the tension. Life's harsh side is real, but so is the kingdom of God.

CHAPTER SIX

What's the Point of All My Striving?

Ecclesiastes 4:4–16

As the 747 sped across the Atlantic, its pilot broke the silence of the flight with an announcement. "Ladies and gentlemen. This is your captain speaking. I'm afraid I have some bad news for you. But I have some good news, too. The bad news is that our radio's not working and we're lost. The good news is that we're making very good time."

Silly as it is, that story illustrates the predicament in which humanity has always found itself. We make ourselves busy with all our work and activity, striving to carve out our niche in the world. We build our little empires, pursue our fortunes, organize our movements, invent our inventions. We seek wealth, power, and esteem.

We make good time. But for what purpose?

Sooner or later we wonder why we work so hard. "What is the point of it all? The more I work, the harder I have to work to keep up with myself. And the faster I run, the less time I have to examine where I'm headed. So what's the point of what I do?"

Solomon would have understood our question. Indeed, I believe he asked it himself as he thought through the meaning of his life. And as he wrote Ecclesiastes, he paused to reflect on what his life had taught him in the areas of success, companionship, and leadership. Since his major goal is still to point out the bankruptcy of the secular philosophy of life by forcing it to be consistent with itself, much of what he says in this section of Ecclesiastes will be colored by that ongoing debate. But at least some of his comments seem to speak more directly from his heart to ours.

SUCCESS

I first met Thomas ten years ago. Young, good-looking, enormously talented, he had strong Christian convictions and was

highly regarded by nearly everyone. But he was also highly motivated to acquire wealth, and before long stories of his shady business dealings and immorality were whispered throughout the
community. For a while it looked as if he was going to get by with
it; he was smart and quick enough on his feet to pull it off if anyone
could.

But then it fell apart. Business. Family. Friends. Eventually his
ambitious drive for success began to destroy everything he valued.

The pursuit of success can be one of life's most disillusioning
goals. By its nature, success is an elusive goal; and even when it is
achieved, it can be frighteningly brief and fleeting. Solomon had
seen the futility of striving for success, and he quickly came to the
essence of the problem it poses.

> Again, I saw that for all toil and every skillful work a man is envied
> by his neighbor. This also is vanity and grasping for the wind (4:4).

Interestingly enough, the Hebrew allows for two meanings for
this verse. Our translation, as well as the King James Version,
declares that one person's success is a cause for envy by others. It is
also possible that the text intends to say that we only pursue success
because we are envious of others' accomplishments: "Then I saw
that all toil and all skill in work come from a man's envy of his
neighbor" (RSV).

Regardless of whether envy comes as the result of someone's
achievement or as an incentive to rise above others, the basic point
is still valid. All of us think highly of ourselves and want to stand
above the crowd; we do not take kindly to being number two in
anything. We want to outshine our neighbors, and we get into the
rat race and beat our heads against the wall trying to outdo others.

Is this true of everybody and everything? Is this the only reason
people strive to achieve? The word *all* is used in two ways in
Scripture; it is used both as "all" in general and as "all" in particular. So when Solomon says, "All toil and every skillful work," most
likely he is painting with his wide brush.

He is saying, "As I look at the world, I see that people are
working themselves to death because they want to outshine their
neighbors. They want to have more than someone else; they are
envious, jealous." He is not necessarily saying that every action we

take has this motive. He is saying that the sum ("all" in the general sense) of our efforts add up to envy. It is vain, empty.

His observation is a good one; it is true. Granted, there are people who work for other reasons. In many areas of the world people work very hard every day just to survive; they work hard all day to get enough money to put food on the table that night. Furthermore, there also are people who do their work diligently simply because they enjoy it; they love their work and want to do it right.

Solomon is not suggesting that we should not work hard or not do our work well. He is speaking of the person who has become immersed in "keeping up with the Joneses" and is working too hard. "I have seen that generally the person who is a workaholic is trying to prove something; he envies his neighbor and wants to get ahead of him."

Of course, there is the opposite extreme. I might add that the fact that Solomon wrote about the lazy individual in the next verse shows he does not mean "all" literally in verse 4.

The fool folds his hands
And consumes his own flesh (4:5).

The lazy man is a fool. When Solomon says that he "consumes his own flesh," he means that he eats what he already has. He looks at the overachiever and says, "Man, that's not for me. I'm just going to sit around and take what's given to me and live off what I already have." So he eats his seed corn. And what he does not seem to realize is that by consuming all he has, he also consumes who he is.

This man reminds us of the wealthy farmer of Jesus' parable. The farmer, too, decided that he could live off what he owned, choosing to "eat, drink, and be merry" (Luke 12:19). Jesus referred to this man as a fool, as Solomon had done centuries earlier when he wrote this passage.

If the workaholic and the drop-out are inadequate role models, what is the answer?

Better is a handful with quietness
Than both hands full, together with toil
and grasping for the wind (4:6).

Solomon says, "Rather than grasping for so much that you have to be a workaholic to get it, be content with less. It is better to have less but enjoy it more."

Our problem is less the high cost of living than it is the cost of high living. We want too much. Solomon says we should scale down our expectations.

A friend recently told me of a visitor from a foreign country who was taken to see one of our large department stores. After a few minutes' time, the man rather incredulously said, "Look at all the things I don't need." First Timothy says, "Godliness with contentment is great gain. . . . But those who desire to be rich fall into temptation and a snare" (6:6,9).

We are to keep our lives in balance. We ought not work so hard to fill both fists. The truth is that our wants will always exceed our grasp anyway, even when we grasp with both fists! Solomon is pleading for a balanced life in which we work as God wants us to work and take what He gives, instead of striving for more.

Solomon has commented on this idea in other places:

Better is a little with the fear of the LORD,
Than great treasure with trouble.
Better is a dinner of herbs where love is,
Than a fatted calf with hatred (Prov. 15:16–17).

Better is a little with righteousness,
Than a fatted calf with hatred (Prov. 15:16–8).

Many homes would be better off working at nurturing love, rather than searching for success. No meal tastes very good without love, but even a meager meal can be good when love is present. And no amount of financial success gained through injustice will ever be as good as less gained righteously. It is a poor life, indeed, that is impoverished in every area except wealth.

But there is more to be considered. Solomon is not finished with this subject.

THE FOLLY OF MATERIALISM

Then I returned, and I saw vanity under the sun:

There is one alone, without companion:
He has neither son nor brother.

Yet there is no end to all his labors,
Nor is his eye satisfied with riches.
But he never asks, "For whom do I toil and deprive myself of good?"
This also is vanity and a grave misfortune (4:7–8).

In order to illustrate the folly of materialistic living, Solomon describes someone who is concerned with success but never asks himself why he is working so hard. Earlier in the book Solomon pointed out that we do not know who will benefit from our work (see 2:18) or whether they will be wise or foolish (see 2:19). But here he is looking at the problem, What shall I do with success?, from a different point of view.

This man has no son or brother—a poetic way of saying he is alone. He has nobody who cares for him or to whom he can leave his wealth. With his single-minded devotion to gain (which Solomon has already assured us he cannot keep for himself), this man probably has no friends, either. He is too busy for friends or family; and as he pursues success after pointless success, he never asks, "For whom do I toil? Why do I deny myself of good?" (see 4:8).

These verses could describe a person who does have a home, wife, and children as easily as not. The truth is that this man's heart is where his treasure is (see Matt. 6:21). If he were to have family and friends, he would not have them for long. He would sacrifice them on the altar of his drive for success.

So even the pursuit of success is pointless. It is vain. Empty. And the secular person will have to look elsewhere to find meaning.

COMPANIONSHIP

Solomon moves from the subject of success at any cost, a philosophy that leads one to be alone and empty, to the subject of companionship. In this section he talks about how much better it is to have companions in life, whether in marriage or in friendships. The person who is tempted to lust after success would do well to listen to these verses, too.

Two are better than one,
Because they have a good reward for their labor.
For if they fall, one will lift up his companion.
But woe to him who is alone when he falls,
For he has no one to help him up.

Again, if two lie down together, they will keep warm;
But how can one be warm alone?
Though one may be overpowered by another,
two can withstand him,
And a threefold cord is not quickly broken (4:9–12).

Solomon gives four rewards of companionship in these verses.
The first reward is that companions can get more done : "Two are
better than one, because they have a good reward for their labor"(v. 9).

Second, good companions know you well enough to know your
faults: "For if they fall, one will lift up his companion. But woe to
him who is alone when he falls, for he has no one to help him up"
(v. 10). Whether it be in marriage or merely in friendship, it is
good to have someone who knows our faults. That person can help
us through the times when we fail and do not know why; he or she
can help us do better next time.

I think it strange that we sometimes become defensive in our
close relationships. If someone criticizes us, we think we have
failed and that the person suddenly dislikes us. But one of the chief
values of our being intimate with someone is so we can learn when
we are wrong. "Faithful are the wounds of a friend" (Prov. 27:6). We
ought to be thankful when someone who knows and loves us
corrects our errors. A companion, one who knows our sins and
weaknesses and is willing to help us overcome them, is part of
God's provision for us.

The third reward of good companionship is warmth. "Again, if
two lie down together, they will keep warm; but how can one be
warm alone?" (v. 11). There is the obvious physical side to this
advantage. Whether the immediate point is that the warmth came
from having an animal to lean against at night while traveling in
the wild Judean highlands (as some commentators believe), or
whether it referred to sleeping in a cold bedroom, one will sleep
warmer if there is a companion.

However, I think Solomon is also talking about emotional
warmth. Every society has had its ways to find physical warmth,
and the rich (which is the context of his discussion) in every time
and place have the least problem with cold weather. When we live
our lives alone, we live in a cold world. All of us need somebody
somewhere—a spouse, a good friend, a counselor.

The fourth value of companionship is strength. "Though one may be overpowered by another, two can withstand him. And a threefold cord is not quickly broken" (v. 12). Solomon is suggesting that we might get in trouble some day; if that happens, we will be better off if we have someone who stands with us as our strength.

My sister is four years older than I. When we were kids, it was quite an advantage to have her around to look out for me. If she was within shouting distance, I never worried about the boys who were older and larger than I; she could take care of them for me. When I was too small to do it on my own, she carried my saxophone to school for me—until the day I hit her from behind with a snowball. She set it down, never to pick it up again! Regardless, I was better off for having someone stronger to look after me, even if I didn't know how to make wise use of her strength!

Solomon says there is strength in having a friend. We might be able to make it on our own; we might not. But if we have someone with us, we are stronger.

Solomon's final statement is interesting. "And a threefold cord is not quickly broken" (v. 12). There is no single illustration that can convey all that statement means. It does illustrate how the love of a man and a woman can be strengthened when a child is born into their family. In view of Solomon's interest in pointing out how desperately we need God in our lives, I believe we should understand the expression to indicate that when God is involved in a relationship, it "is not quickly broken." That is, where God is *allowed* to be God in a marriage, it does not become broken. It might if He is there but has been put on the shelf. This principle holds true in all relationships. If we allow God to be God in them, wholeness and good will result. If we shelve Him, we deprive ourselves of our strongest resource.

There are two reasons for making an issue of this. First, we must not try to go through life alone. Whether we are married or single, have loads of friends or few, we need one another. Christians of all ages need the support of other Christians. I recommend that every Christian become a part of a support group; I have benefited from one for many years. We get together to share our joys and our burdens, and we stay in touch with one another to be sure we do not let anyone down. We need each other.

The second reason for making this an issue is that we need to see there is a price to pay for lasting companionship. Verse 9 uses the word *better;* in fact, Solomon uses it twenty-one times in Ecclesiastes. It is "better" to have companionship; most of us would agree with that. But we must be prepared to pay the price for good friends and good marriages.

When we enter into marriage or make friends or develop a close relationship with other Christians, we lose our independence. We joke when a friend is about to marry, "Oh, you're going to bite the dust. Marriage is a ball . . . and chain!" However, there is a touch of truth to this joking. If we try to keep our independence and enter into marriage, we will not have a good marriage. If we think we do not have to take the ideas or feelings or needs of our spouse or our friends or our Christian brothers and sisters into consideration, we will not have true companionship—or friendship—with them. "In lowliness of mind let each esteem others better than himself. Let each of you look out not only for his own interests, but also for the interests of others" (Phil. 2:3–4).

Whether it is in marriage, friendship, or the church, we have to be ready to listen to others ("This person's ideas might be better than mine"), ready to learn their interests ("There might be something good for me in it"), ready to look out for their needs ("I am God's neighbor for this person"), ready to adjust to their pace and style ("Two of us cannot walk together if we walk at different speeds").

Yes, companionship is better, but there is a price, and it must be paid every day. Is it worth it? You bet! But we must not forget the price, or it will no longer be good.

LEADERSHIP

Being a king, Solomon had ample opportunity to think about leadership, especially in the political realm.

> Better is a poor and wise youth
> Than an old and foolish king who will be admonished no more.
> For he comes out of prison to be king,
> Although he was born poor in his kingdom.
> I saw all the living who walk under the sun;
> They were with the second youth who stands in his place.
> There was no end of all the people over whom he was made king;

Yet those who come afterward will not rejoice in him.
Surely this also is vanity and grasping for the wind (4:13–16).

Solomon had seen the comings and goings of leaders. Even his own experience had taught him that popularity is frequently short-lived; that which endears a leader to the masses can alienate them from him just as quickly.

Solomon seems to be comparing two kinds of kings. One has been on the throne a long time. Regardless of whether he ruled well in his earlier years, he has become so accustomed to power that he forgets that he needs advice. He becomes a poor leader. Then a young man comes along, only this young man built his support at the grass roots level. Suddenly, everyone is following the new king and the old one is replaced. This certainly sounds "better" (v. 13). But wait! "Yet those who come afterward will not rejoice in him" (v. 16). The next generation will reject him. So it goes with leadership.

In Chapter 1 we noted that one of Solomon's key points in Ecclesiastes is that nothing is permanent. Here he gives us another illustration of life's impermanence. Who, after all, has more security than a king? He has all the power of a kingdom at his disposal. And yet, in this illogical world in which we live, even the people who should be able to control events are unable to do so. They, too, become victims of life's fickle fortunes.

Time and familiarity have a way of eroding popularity. Not many leaders stay at the top for long. Politically, most of the recent presidents of the United States were acclaimed when they were elected but fell out of favor before their terms were half-completed. Few managers of major league teams or coaches of the top college teams stay at their job throughout their careers. The people who shouted "Hosanna" to Jesus also called for His crucifixion.

Both of the kings Solomon presents came to the same end. Popular acclaim does not last, and those who aspire to positions of leadership would be wise to remember that. It does not seem to make a great deal of difference whether one is a good ruler or not; those who come along later "will not rejoice in him."

This does not have to be as pessimistic as it sounds. Remember, Solomon is addressing his words to one who chooses to live his life without considering how God relates to it. He is pointing out what any fair-minded person can observe for himself. What Solomon wants his secular-minded friend—and us—to see is that even at its highest levels, life is insecure. We cannot depend upon anything that is of this world. And if our highest dreams turn out to be nightmares when God is not a part of them, what, then, should those of us who do not enjoy positions of power, popularity, and acclaim expect?

Leadership—power, money, influence, acclaim—is not where satisfaction is to be found. One cannot depend on leadership, anymore than one can depend on any other form of worldly success. We should be thankful for whatever blessings we have, but we should also remember that they are gifts entrusted to us. They are temporary, fleeting.

Only the One who gives these gifts will not fail us. He is satisfying and permanent. Everything from Him is a gift, and with Him there is no fickleness. In Him there is no vanity, either; indeed, in Him there is great profit, great gain.

CHAPTER SEVEN
Be Real When You Worship

Ecclesiastes 5:1–9

On the surface, it is hard to imagine how worship, of all things, could be "vain"—empty and worthless. Yet that is the picture Solomon paints in this section of Ecclesiastes, that of worship gone to seed and now become empty and worthless. This worship is "vain" because of the insincerity with which it is offered and by the thoughtlessness by which it is motivated. It was a problem in Solomon's time; it is with us today.

How many times I have heard people say they do not attend any church because it is not meaningful to them. I believe people when they tell me that. Obviously, if worship had meant much to them, they would have continued. Ironically, we get out of worship what we invest in it; and even the best preacher in the world cannot "feed" people who come to the hour of worship with closed mouths!

But not everyone who finds worship to be empty of meaning drops out of the church. Some keep coming, regularly or irregularly, for whatever reasons. They are the people to whom Solomon addressed these remarks. He was concerned by the problems created by empty worship, and in looking around himself he realized it was rooted in the very reason one worships. Does one worship God because He is the Holy One who ought to be loved and praised? Does one worship God for the emotional thrill of warmth or ecstasy that comes from being in His presence? Does one worship God in order to be seen worshiping God?

As Solomon looked around, he realized that the problem of the secular mind was not confined to people who lived as though God were unimportant in their lives. Many of the people who worshiped regularly at the temple were equally secular in their approach to God. They were worshiping themselves, not God. They were making a joke out of worship.

So Solomon protested, "Your worship is a farce. It is an exercise in futility. You drag your body to worship, but your mind is in another world. You listen with half an ear, you sing halfheartedly, and you plan out your next week's work while the Word of God is being taught. You give nothing to God when you worship. You expect nothing. And that is what you get—nothing!"

Because Solomon understood the human heart so well, he suggested several steps we can take to insure that our worship is fresh and meaningful. Interestingly enough, he listed them in chronological order—before, during, and after the worship hour.

I believe he handled the subject this way because he knew that our failure to worship God properly is rooted in our being unprepared to worship, our lack of attention to what is happening during worship, and our inability or unwillingness to follow through on our commitments once we leave the sanctuary.

BEFORE WORSHIP

Walk prudently when you go to the house of God (5:1).

The Revised Standard Version reads, "Guard your steps." Solomon was thinking of the temple in Jerusalem when he wrote of "the house of God." It was the place where Israel worshiped God; when we worship with other Christians, we normally worship at the church. Regardless, we can also worship God by ourselves in our "room," as Jesus said (Matt. 6:6).

Solomon says, "Walk prudently. Guard your steps." We should give our minds to our worship long before we arrive at the place for worship. We ought to prepare ourselves so that when we arrive, our worship will be deliberate, grateful, and heartfelt.

The gospel of John says, "But the hour is coming, and now is, when the true worshipers will worship the Father in spirit and truth; for the Father is seeking such to worship Him" (John 4:23). God is delighted when we worship Him; but He is offended when our worship is casual or haphazard.

There are several examples of careless worship mentioned in the Bible. In Leviticus 15 God warns the Israelites not to come to the tabernacle to worship when they are unclean and have not prepared themselves, "lest they die in their uncleanness when they defile My tabernacle" (v. 31).

In Hebrews chapter 10 it says that in preparing a place in heaven for us and in preparing us to worship Him there, God went to the extreme of giving His Son in death so that we could "enter the Holiest by the blood of Jesus" (v. 19). God's holiness demands that we prepare ourselves to worship and that we do not take it casually. If our worship is going to be authentic and fruitful, it must begin before we arrive.

There are a number of steps we can take in preparation for our worship of God. First, we can anticipate the hour. We ought to cultivate an anticipation for worship. If Jesus Christ is really our Lord and He means more to us than anything else, then we should come to this hour with anticipation. The hour when we worship together should be the high point of our week.

Second, we ought to pray for the hour of worship. We ought to be in intercessory prayer throughout the week, but we ought to approach the hour of worship with two prayers in mind. We ought to pray, "Speak to each person in this service, Lord" and "Speak to me first." That is why, for instance, in the church I pastor, I meet with the elders of the church at 7:10 A.M. for prayer. It is important.

If we do not prepare our hearts for worship, we might not worship God "in spirit and truth" (John 4:23), and we might cheat ourselves of a meaningful encounter with the Lord. When we do not "get much out of it" during worship, it almost always is due to our failure to prepare our hearts. Even the heaviest rain will run off parched, hard ground. We will miss the blessings of God when our hearts are not soft and pliable, and we need to prepare ourselves for worship with prayer.

It is interesting that some people get a lot from every worship experience, while others seldom appreciate the privilege they have of worshiping the Lord. Why is it that one person is moved by God during a worship service, while another complains about not being fed? Is it a matter of being prepared? Does it come from confusing worship with entertainment? We should be able to worship God and have a fresh encounter with Him even if the organ is broken, the pastor has laryngitis, and the choir is on vacation!

Third, we need to prepare ourselves physically. Perhaps I am more aware of this because I am a pastor and often preach four times on Sunday, but I do not know how someone who is physically exhausted on Sunday morning can worship God in mind, in body, or in spirit. We need to be sure we are not physically exhausted, emotionally distracted, or mentally preoccupied with events in our lives. We should also be prudent about how we spend our Saturday evenings.

We want to be ready to worship God.

DURING WORSHIP

Solomon has some strong words for the person who has come to worship in a casual fashion.

> . . . draw near to hear rather than to give the sacrifice of fools, for they do not know that they do evil.

> Do not be rash with your mouth,
> And let not your heart utter anything hastily before God.
> For God is in heaven, and you on earth;
> Therefore let your words be few.
> For a dream comes through much activity,
> And a fool's voice is known by his many words (5:1–3).

"Draw near to hear" means: "Come with open, tender hearts. Come with listening ears. Don't come to tell God what to do." We can tell God what we want, but we must come near to listen to Him. That is better than to offer "the sacrifice of fools" (v. 1). The sacrifice of fools is empty words. The fool has forgotten both who God is and who he himself is. He takes liberties with the grace and patience of God. A fool is such a fool that he does not know that what he is doing is evil (see v. 1).

What is it that a fool does when he "worships"? We have to look at what Solomon tells us *not* to do to see what the fool was doing: "Do not be rash with your mouth,/And let not your heart utter anything hastily before God./For God is in heaven, and you on earth;/Therefore let your words be few" (v. 2). There is a big difference between God and us. The fool forgets that difference when he worships. He is hasty with his words, not thinking them through or praying them with sincerity.

When Solomon says, "let your words be few," he is not speaking so much about long prayers as about pretentious praying. God cannot stand our pouring out empty phrases in worship, but He does honor persistent prayer (see Luke 11:5–8).

In Genesis 32:22-29 we read of Jacob's wrestling with God and declaring that he would not let go until God blessed him. And God blessed him. God is not against long or persistent prayers if they mean something to the one raising them. He wants us to spend much time in prayer with Him, but He does not want empty, vain words that do not come from the heart.

We know how that is. When we talk with someone whose mind is somewhere else and the whole conversation becomes an extended vocalized pause, we may be insulted. We excuse ourselves as quickly as we can. This kind of verbal doodling irritates us. It irritates God, too. He wants sincere prayers.

Solomon has already discussed the fool in Ecclesiastes (2:14, 15, 16, 19; 4:5, 13), and he will return to it again later (6:8; 7:6, 17, 25; 10:2, 3, 12, 14, 15). Nowhere does he speak more directly about the consequence of being a fool than here: the fool does his folly naturally. "A fool's voice is known by his many words" (5:3). He cannot help himself.

When Solomon compares foolish worship with a dream-filled night, he touches on something most people understand. Nearly everyone has had hectic days when there was so much happening that the night was filled with tossing and turning and strange dreams. I know one man who cannot sleep for hours after going to an exciting basketball game, even though it has been nearly twenty years since he has played in a serious game himself.

There is something about us that makes it hard for us to shut off our minds after a hectic or exciting day, and so we dream dreams. It happens naturally. Just as a busy day causes dreams, so a fool causes empty words. Where you have one, you have the other. We ought not play the fool in our worship.

AFTER WORSHIP

How many times I have heard someone castigate the hypocrites in the church! Where else would we like to see them? The hypocrites *should* be at church. However, hypocrisy is a serious issue in the church; probably most Christians have heard more on this subject than we care to hear. Solomon had something important to say about hypocritical worship.

> When you make a vow to God, do not delay to pay it;
> For He has no pleasure in fools.
> Pay what you have vowed.
> It is better not to vow than to vow and not pay (5:4–5).

I like the way Solomon understands us. He does not say, "*If* you make a vow to God." He says, "*When* you make a vow to God." We all make vows, or commitments. Solomon understood that. He also knew that we need to be as prompt in keeping our vows as we are in making them.

We are not to delay in paying our vows. "Delay" is the key word here. No one makes a vow with the intention of breaking it, but it is easy to make our vows, walk out of the place of worship, and set them aside, assuming we will fulfill them later. But all too easily tomorrow becomes next week, and next week becomes next month, and next month becomes next year—or never. The consequence is that many Christians live defeated lives because they made vows to God and have not kept them.

In another place Solomon wrote, "It is a snare for a man to devote rashly something as holy, and afterward to reconsider his vows" (Prov. 20:25). It is easy to make a vow in a sincere moment and then avoid it once we have had time to consider its cost.

It is interesting that even early in Israel's history, allowance had been made for this human weakness. In Deuteronomy it is written: "But if you abstain from vowing, it shall not be sin to you. That which has gone from your lips you shall keep and perform, for you voluntarily vowed to the LORD your God what you have promised with your mouth" (23:22–23). We would be better off not to make any vows than to make them and look for excuses to avoid them.

There is a story in the New Testament that describes an incident that happened in the early church. Ananias and Sapphira sold some property, apparently to keep a vow they had made; but when the time came to pay it, they withheld part of it but presented the rest as if it were the entire amount they had received. They both were struck dead by the Lord because they withheld what they pretended to give to the Lord (see Acts 5:1–11). It is a serious business when we make vows to God, and we ought not make them lightly.

Nothing hardens a heart or sears a conscience as much as being brought to the point of melting and then cooling to the same old shape. "It is better not to vow than to vow and not pay" (5:5).

Do not let your mouth cause your flesh to sin, nor say before the messenger of God that it was an error. Why should God be angry at your excuse and destroy the work of your hands? For in the multitude of dreams and many words there is also vanity. But fear God (5:6–7).

The people who make Christian plaques should make one of "Do not let your mouth cause your flesh to sin" (5:6). I can think of many applications for that statement, but its context is the vow we have made. We ought not let ourselves sin in making our commitments to the Lord by trying to excuse ourselves from keeping them. "Oh, that was a mistake, Lord. I really shouldn't have made that vow." We ought not try to escape our vows.

The tragic breakdown of marriages in our time is an illustration of our hypocritical worship. Marriage is a covenant; both partners take vows before God to keep that covenant (see Mal. 2:14). To break one's marriage covenant is to break a vow made before God as surely as is failing to give Him the gift we have promised.

It is a serious business to avoid our vows to the Lord. The question "Why should God be angry at your excuse and destroy the works of your hands?" (v. 6) presents frightening possibilities. The costs of not keeping our vows may become greater than the costs of paying them. This, too, is vanity.

We are not to dream about what we are going to do; we are to do it (see v. 7). If we never make any commitments to the Lord, we are not going to grow with Him. We need to make our commitments. But they should be sober, deliberate, thoughtful, reverent. And we should keep them so that our worship does not become just one more vanity in a vain world!

It is a great privilege we have to worship God. It is also a serious business. We ought to come with hearts that are prepared. We ought to be sober in the commitments we make. We ought to do what we promise God we will do. This is what God expects from true worship.

It will give us great joy when we offer it to Him!

CHAPTER EIGHT

Why Wealth Cannot Make Us Happy

Ecclesiastes 5:10–20

One of Solomon's first statements in Ecclesiastes was, "What profit has a man from all his labor?" (1:3). It should not surprise us, then, that eventually he would talk about profit and its pursuit. Centuries later, the apostle Paul would declare, "For the love of money is a root of all kinds of evil, for which some have strayed from the faith in their greediness, and pierced themselves through with many sorrows" (1 Tim. 6:10).

Money, and the love of it, is a basic motivation of life "under the sun," that is, in the observable world. Successful businessmen know that this is true. Certainly advertisers know it. It is no accident that when the obviously successful person on the television screen discreetly leans toward a friend and says, "My broker is E. F. Hutton, and E. F. Hutton says . . ." everyone drops whatever he is doing to eavesdrop.

Profit is important to us. We crave it. Sometimes we even live and die for it.

Solomon was the wisest man who had ever lived (see 1 Kin. 4:29–34). He would not have had to have been all that wise, though, to know that men and women crave wealth. He knew that many people live for wealth; but his wisdom helped him see that most of us do not realize how little happiness and satisfaction it will bring us. So he challenges his readers to take an honest look at the vanity (the emptiness) of riches. As he writes, he helps us see the unsatisfying nature of wealth. Later on he discloses where we can find a satisfying life.

THE UNSATISFACTORY NATURE OF WEALTH

The irony of wealth is that it is not necessary to have a lot of money to love it. Some people believe "the vanity of riches" refers to rich people. Yet, it may or may not refer to the rich. When we talk about the love of money, we are talking about people at every level of income. Some of the world's most materialistic people do not have two nickels to rub together. And frankly, some of the wealthy people I know seem to hold it very loosely and do not appear to be preoccupied with money.

When I was in seminary, one of the seniors preached a sermon in which he talked about the subtle dangers of materialism. Laughing, he illustrated his point that you can love wealth without having it; he told an interesting story on himself. He had an old Pontiac; it might have been worth $100.00, but I would not have given that much for it. He said, "I realized how subtle materialism can be one day when I found myself looking at that car, with pride and affection!"

My reaction was that materialism can be not only deceptive but also irrational!

In talking about the love of money, we are not talking about people of any particular economic level. However, we need to remember that as our goods increase, we are probably in greater danger of growing attached to them or of selfishly striving to attain more regardless of the cost. It is important that we do not allow money to become a substitute for God in our lives or try to make it do something it will never be able to do.

One of the best things that ever happened to me was to be born into my parents' family. My parents were a beautiful model to us children of how to handle material blessings. We never had a lot of money. My father was a pastor; and while the clergy were considerably less well-paid in those days than they are today, we never suffered any deprivation. Money was never an issue; my parents believed God would provide for us. He did. But more importantly, they taught us that financial success was not nearly as profitable as knowing God. Because they had trusted God to provide for them, they were grateful for everything He had given them. They were free to concentrate their efforts on loving their children and building a happy home.

We kids thought we had it made, and we did. We knew that Mom and Dad loved us, and they raised us to know that God loved us. They knew better than to try to make money into something it never can be.

It is "profitable" for us to understand the true value of wealth. We can be grateful that Solomon gave us several insights into its nature. In doing so, he proclaims that living for wealth is unsatisfying and self-defeating. There are several reasons why this is true.

WE ALWAYS WANT MORE

1. *The more we gain, the more we desire.* The pursuit of wealth is much like an addiction. It feeds on itself and will consume the person who is not careful.

> He who loves silver will not be satisfied with silver;
> Nor he who loves abundance, with increase.
> This also is vanity (5:10).

Solomon has observed something nearly everyone can see. When material things are the focus of life, our desires always outrun our ability to acquire or to enjoy. I am told that someone once asked John D. Rockefeller, "How much money do you want?" Mr. Rockefeller answered, "Just a little bit more." That is how it is with wealth. No matter how much we have, we want just a little bit more.

I live in the midst of a wealthy community. Some of the wealthiest and most influential people in Minnesota live within walking distance of our church. I see the emptiness that living for wealth can bring. Of course, I also know some wealthy people whose lives radiate joy and happiness. One of the big differences is in the importance they attach to their wealth. That is why both the wealthy and the poor can suffer equally from the love-of-money disease.

It works like this: God has placed eternity within our hearts (see 3:11). This means that at the core of who we are, God has planted a hunger for the Eternal that nothing else can satisfy. So when we substitute anything for God (the Bible calls this sin by its name—idolatry), we create a dangerous imbalance in our lives. We become unfocused. Because of the way God made us, underneath everything we have a great hunger for Him. However, we are easily confused by the temptation to put something else at the center; in this case that temptation is money. That is why we become unhappy whenever money becomes too important; we become out-of-focus with what God created us to be. Instead of the gain which the love of money promises, we are left with emptiness!

A life built on the pursuit of wealth will not bring satisfaction, no matter how much a person obtains. It is vanity. It is empty.

THE MORE WE HAVE, THE MORE WE SPEND

2. *Our expenses keep up with our income.* Notice how Solomon describes the fate of the person who becomes financially successful:

When goods increase,
They increase who eat them;
So what profit have the owners
Except to see them with their eyes? (5:11).

As our wealth increases, so do the people who try to get their fingers in our pie! There is an interesting passage in Isaiah that illustrates this principle. A man named Eliakim is promised that he will become an important official, but he is warned that the hangers-on will become a terrible burden. Picturing him as a peg on a wall, Isaiah declares, "They will hang on him all the glory of his father's house, the offspring and the issue, all vessels of small quantity, from the cups to all the pitchers" (22:24). His success would be a burden instead of a joy.

One of the frustrations that comes with financial success is the reality that we then need people to manage and protect our wealth. We need lawyers and accountants and managers and experts of all sorts. We also attract the very people who will take our wealth away from us if we let them! That is one of the reasons we need the counsel of experts.

So Solomon looks at all this and asks an interesting question: Is it really worth the effort? If wealth brings the parasites out of the woodwork, and if we will need assistance to manage what we have, what's the point of having it? What good is it, other than to watch it as it slips through our fingers?

Earlier, Solomon had pointed out the futility of achievement: no matter how successful we are, we will not be remembered (see 2:16) and someone else will enjoy what we have built (see 2:21). Here he says that the truth is even worse than that: wealth will bring us burdens, and we will not gain nearly as much as we think we will. Other than the enjoyment of watching it come and go, there is not much gain, only prestige. The hangers-on will do their best to eat us out of house and home.

ADDITIONAL WEALTH MEANS ADDITIONAL WORRY

3. *Wealth may bring sleepless nights.* I am amazed at how many people cannot sleep at night because of tension. They have so many responsibilities or they are working so hard to become successful or they are so worried about the future that they cannot sleep. Wealth, especially our concern for it, often results in insomnia.

> The sleep of a laboring man is sweet,
> Whether he eats little or much;
> But the abundance of the rich will not permit him to sleep (5:12).

The laboring man may not bring home a large paycheck, but he works hard and his sleep is sweet. Why? The first reason is that he has worked hard and his body is tired. The second is that he has little cause for worry. He does not have to worry about what the stock market will look like in the morning, and he does not have to worry about keeping his subordinates productive and the business profitable. He had a job to do, and he did it. At the end of the day he ate whatever food he could and slept peacefully.

The wealthy man did not enjoy the same rest. His sleeplessness is not the insomnia that comes from too much work to do (see 2:23). Rather, because he has more than he needs, he is able to indulge himself and is more likely to eat and drink too much and do too little physical work. The fact that his wealth brings him greater burdens does not help him, either. As a result, he has trouble sleeping and tosses and turns throughout the night (see 5:12).

We understand what Solomon means when he talks about too much food and too little physical exercise. He could easily be describing our culture. It is no wonder we find it necessary to join health clubs and fitness centers to undo the damages of our prosperous, sedentary lives.

WEALTH DOESN'T GUARANTEE SECURITY

4. *Our wealth may vanish.*

> There is a severe evil which I have seen under the sun:
> Riches kept for their owner to his hurt.
> But those riches perish through misfortune;
> When he begets a son, there is nothing in his hand (5:13–14).

It is possible that Solomon is talking about a miserly use of wealth, but I think instead that he is referring to a business venture that went sour. The word translated "misfortune" in verse 14 is the same word that obviously refers to work in other verses in Ecclesiastes (e.g., 1:13; 3:10; 4:3; 8:16). Solomon's point is that the man's venture went so bad that at the end of his life he had "no gain" to give to his heir.

This man had two problems. First, he was broke. This was bad enough. But the tragedy is that he had toiled and had been vexed (see v. 17) the entire time he was creating his wealth (like the man in 2:23). His work created so much pressure for him that he was miserable while he gained his wealth. The irony is that his life was ruined twice over, once in gaining his wealth and again in losing it.

In Proverbs, Solomon commented on the impermanence of wealth, its transcience. "A man with an evil eye hastens after riches,/And does not consider that poverty will come upon him" (28:22). Solomon is not necessarily saying that wealth is ill-gotten or that our wealth will vanish. However, he is saying that it could vanish. We all have known or heard of people whose wealth has evaporated almost overnight. Earlier in my ministry a man came to me with that very story. He had been wealthy, but had lost every penny he had. The possibility that wealth might vanish is always present, and that is one of the simple realities of this world that makes the love of wealth an unwise, unsatisfying base upon which to build our lives.

Solomon has one more observation to make about the unsatisfactory nature of riches.

TRUST IN GOD, NOT RICHES

5. *We cannot take our wealth with us.* We know this, but we are quick to forget it.

> As he came from his mother's womb, naked shall he return,
> To go as he came;
> And he shall take nothing from his labor
> Which he may carry away in his hand.
> And this also is a severe evil,
> That just exactly as he came, so shall he go.
> And what profit has he who has labored for the wind?
> All his days he also eats in darkness,
> And he has much sorrow and sickness and anger (5:15–17).

There is no need to overwork the point. When my life is over, exactly what will I take away with me?

Nothing.

Solomon uses a clever phrase in verse 16. He asks, "And what profit has he who has labored for the wind?" Earlier in Ecclesiastes he has commented that he has "seen all the works that are done under the sun; and indeed, all is vanity and grasping for the wind" (1:14). Now he says that we have even *worked* "for the wind."

To work for wealth is like working for the wind. Just as you get it, you lose it. It is gone, like a vapor, a puff. Regardless of whether one ever suffers the losses described in verses 13 and 14 and regardless of whether one ever amasses a fortune, in the end we have nothing material to show for our lives.

We can take nothing with us where we are going.

So why should we be like the miser? Why "eat in darkness?" (This may be a figure of speech for the gloom of a miserable life lived for riches only.) Why fill one's life with "sorrow and sickness and anger" by striving for a wealth that we will ultimately lose anyway?

This is a serious question. It cuts across every economic level, and it points to the basic futility of a life lived for wealth, "for the wind." It is vanity. It is a miserable lot. Vanity of vanities!

It would be better to remember the words of the apostle Paul to

Timothy: "Command those who are rich in this present age not to be haughty, nor to trust in uncertain riches but in the living God, who gives us richly all things to enjoy" (1 Tim. 6:17). Solomon has more to say on this subject, and he moves on to declare where we can find satisfaction and joy.

SATISFACTION IS A GIFT FROM GOD

Recently I ran across an article written by an older pastor whom I have known most of my adult life. In reflecting upon his life, he wrote, "If I had my ministry to do over again, I would seek to enjoy it more." We are to enjoy our lives, not to seek wealth. Solomon expressed it this way:

> Here is what I have seen: It is good and fitting for one to eat and drink, and to enjoy the good of all his labor in which he toils under the sun all the days of his life which God gives him; for it is his heritage. As for every man to whom God has given riches and wealth, and given him power to eat of it, to receive his heritage and rejoice in his labor—this is the gift of God. For he will not dwell unduly on the days of his life, because God keeps him busy with the joy of his heart (5:18–20).

At this point Solomon begins to give his prescription for achieving satisfaction. At first it seems as if he is simply advocating a return to a simple lifestyle of enjoying the good things in life. He says it is "good and fitting" to consume the fruits of our work. But then Solomon introduces the key to our search for satisfaction—God. God gives what we need—food, drink, wealth, joy. All of this "is the gift of God" (5:19). The Revised Standard Version reminds us that God gives us the "power" to enjoy them. God is both the satisfaction we seek and the source of all the good we enjoy.

Solomon has been conducting an experiment in this book. He is asking the secular-minded individual to look at life honestly and consider the ultimate implications of his own philosophy. Occasionally, Solomon lets his own beliefs come through strongly, and this is one of those places. He is not content to report vividly what everyone can see; he decides to give us a glimpse of what God has shown him.

Solomon has decided that no matter what happens, he is going to be grateful. He is going to enjoy his work (being a king sounds like a pretty great job, anyway!). He is going to enjoy his food; he is going to enjoy his relaxation—he is going to enjoy everything. It is important to realize that he is speaking here as a person of faith; he is showing the reader the principles by which he lives and the reader should live. He has already warned us that the pursuit of wealth will not make us happy. Now he tells us simply to enjoy life.

It is a comfort to know that the ability to enjoy life is a gift from God (see 5:19). We do not just decide to enjoy life and then sit back and do it. Thus, he repeats the message of chapter 2: "For God gives wisdom and knowledge and joy to a man who is good in His sight" (2:26). Joy is God's gift.

Solomon's summary of the situation is beautiful. He says that the person who loves God and puts the values of His kingdom first will not be discouraged when he discovers that wealth will not bring him happiness; he already knows it. He has already found happiness. God will keep him busy with the true desires of his heart. There is a surprise in all this, though—the desire of his heart is to know and love and serve God. His heart's desire is not to pursue something that is a poor substitute for the real thing.

The one who loves God "with the joy of his heart" enjoys life as God gives it and is grateful for every moment. Looking back over the years, only one verdict is appropriate: "It's been good. My life has been so good."

And not one morsel of striving makes it that way!

CHAPTER NINE

The Questionable Value of Wealth

Ecclesiastes 6:1–12

My sister was old enough to have boyfriends, and I was just old enough to be a pest about it. One Sunday afternoon she had a date with a boy who was supposed to leave for home a little before three o'clock in the afternoon. However, not long before he arrived, another boyfriend unexpectedly called, and she told him he could come over around three. Three o'clock came, and boyfriend number one had not yet left.

I was thoroughly enjoying my sister's dilemma. There she sat, nervously talking with one boyfriend in the living room, knowing full well that the other one was due at any moment. Taking advantage of the situation, I swaggered to the middle of the room, stopped, and looked my sister in the eye. "What are you going to do now, Phyllis?" I said with a laugh.

Phyllis's situation on that Sunday afternoon seems funny now. It certainly was not funny to her then, though. And the dilemma in which she found herself left her with apparently no good choices.

Modern man, too, is in a dilemma. Billboards, television, and the conversation of nearly everyone we know all blend together to proclaim, "Money is where it's at. Money is number one. It's everything!"

But is it?

In the previous chapter we discovered that wealth is essentially unsatisfying. It does not deliver what it promises. Solomon explored five areas in which wealth disappoints us: the more we gain, the more we desire; our expenses keep up with our income; wealth may bring us worry and sleeplessness; it may vanish like the fog; we cannot take it with us when we leave this life. All this is quite different from the picture that our culture paints of what wealth will deliver.

Solomon then went on to discuss where satisfaction *does* originate (see 5:18). It comes from God alone; it is a gift. The irony is that we strive hard for it but will have to give up our search if we hope to experience it.

Solomon has not finished with the subject of wealth, and he continues to discuss it in terms of its uncertainties, its unknowns. He says, "We don't know enough to know if wealth will be good for us." Far too many of us crave wealth and assume its possession will make us happy and fulfilled. "Not necessarily so," says Solomon. He goes on to discuss three questions about wealth that none of us can answer.

WHO KNOWS WHETHER WE WILL ENJOY WEALTH?

In chapter 5 we were told that the "power" (RSV) to enjoy God's gifts is itself a gift. Here we begin to realize that this power might not be given to us. There are so many unknowns in life; and Solomon invites his secular-minded reader—and all who read his book—to look at this question carefully.

> There is an evil which I have seen under the sun, and it is common among men: A man to whom God has given riches and wealth and honor, so that he lacks nothing for himself of all he desires; yet God does not give him power to eat of it, but a foreigner consumes it. This is vanity, and it is an evil affliction. If a man begets a hundred children and lives many years, so that the days of his years are many, but his soul is not satisfied with goodness, or indeed he has no burial, I say that a stillborn child is better than he—for it comes in vanity and departs in darkness, and its name is covered with darkness. Though it has not seen the sun or known anything, this has more rest than that man, even if he lives a thousand years twice over—but has not seen goodness. Do not all go to one place? (6:1–6).

Earlier in Ecclesiastes Solomon wrote: "There is nothing better for a man than that he should eat and drink, and that his soul should enjoy good in his labor. This also, I saw, was from the hand of God" (2:24). The Revised Standard Version continues in verse 25 with "for apart from him who can eat or who can have enjoyment?" If God does not give us the ability to enjoy life, we will be unable to enjoy it. Later, he also wrote, "And also that every man should eat and drink and enjoy the good of all his labor—it is a gift of God" (3:13). Again he tells us that God wants us to enjoy life.

In chapter 5 Solomon repeats his assertion: "Here is what I have seen: It is good and fitting for one to eat and drink, and to enjoy the good of all his labor in which he toils under the sun in all the days of his life which God gives him; for it is his heritage" (v. 18).

What Solomon wants to communicate is clear: God wants us to enjoy life. He wants us to enjoy the material things we possess. They are for our pleasure and joy.

I love to come home in the midst of a Minnesota winter after a long day at work, sit down in a comfortable chair, put up my feet, and thank God for a good chair, a footstool, and a warm furnace. Frankly, I never thought to thank God for a furnace until I moved to Minnesota! But I firmly believe God intends for us to enjoy our furnaces, footstools, and chairs, as well as everything else we use.

Will we? Nobody knows for sure.

"There is an evil which I have seen under the sun, and it is common among men: a man to whom God has given riches and wealth and honor, so that he lacks nothing for himself of all he desires; yet God does not give him the power to eat of it [RSV, "enjoy"], but a foreigner consumes it" (6:1–2). The evil is that even though God has given this man the power to own these possessions, He has not given him the power to enjoy them. The cause for this failure could be war, sickness, oppression, or whatever. Regardless, God has not allowed him to enjoy his riches. Surely this is a "vain" and "evil affliction" to the heart of one whose vision is limited to this life only.

Following this, Solomon lists some of the things, other than wealth, that have great value to people. "If a man begets a hundred children" (in those days a hundred children would have been considered a great joy; they were an economic asset to the family) "and lives many years, so that the days of his years are many" (in verse 6 he says that even if you live "a thousand years twice over"—two thousand years!), "or indeed he has no burial" (in those days the manner in which you were buried was a statement about the significance of your life), "I say that a stillborn child is better than he" (6:3).

Several years ago when I pastored a church in the Los Angeles area, I happened to drive by the Forest Lawn Cemetery. Two delightful elderly women were my passengers. One was in her nineties, and the other was nearly her age. Just as we passed Forest Lawn, an airplane flew over us on its way to the Burbank airport. One of the women peered at the cemetery through the smog and in a serious voice declared, "I wouldn't want to be buried there. Too noisy."

We joke about burial, but it was no joking matter in ancient Israel. Repeatedly, the Old Testament refers to the ignominy of death without burial. For instance, when Jeremiah the prophet uttered the judgment of the Lord against Jehoiakim, the king of Judah, the greatest insult he hurled against him touched on this issue.

> "They shall not lament for him,
> Saying, 'Alas, my brother!'
>   or 'Alas, my sister!'
> They shall not lament for him,
> Saying, 'Alas, master!'
>   or 'Alas, his glory!'
> He shall be buried with the burial
>   of a donkey,
> Dragged and cast out beyond the gates
>   of Jerusalem" (Jer. 22:18–19).

Isaiah also refers to the horrible circumstance of not having one's body rest in the grave.

> "All the kings of the nations,
> All of them, sleep in glory,
> Everyone in his own house;
> But you are cast out of your grave
> Like an abominable branch,
> Like the garment of those who are slain,
> Thrust through with a sword,
> Who go down to the stones of the pit,
> Like a corpse trodden under foot" (Is. 14:18–19).

In both cases, the horror of being unburied or having one's grave vandalized is a matter of the greatest concern. To suffer either would be a disgrace.

Solomon says, "Look at that man. He has all this wealth and all those children, and yet he is unhappy; and his children don't care enough about him to give him a decent burial. A stillborn child is better off than he is." (Job 3:16 and Psalm 58:8 also refer to instances where someone would have been better off to have been stillborn; this is a figurative way to express evil experienced at its worst.) Here is a man who has every success anyone could want, and yet his wealth has not brought him enjoyment.

In verses 4–6 Solomon reminds us that all of us die, rich and poor alike. His point is that since we all live only once and then die, it would be tragic to fail to enjoy our lives, regardless of the reason. What good is wealth if we are not able to enjoy ourselves while we have it? And since we cannot know in advance whether or not we will enjoy wealth once it is ours, why pursue it? Since we only go around once in life, why not accept the Providence of God and make the most of what He will give us if we will accept it!

WHO KNOWS WHETHER WEALTH WILL BE SATISFYING?

Solomon touches on a sore nerve when he moves to this question. Since chapter 5, verse 10, he has been discussing it in one way or another. He becomes quite pointed here.

At first glance it seems as if his comments are exaggerated.

> All the labor of man is for his mouth,
> And yet the soul is not satisfied (6:7).

He made a similar observation in the Book of Proverbs: "The person who labors, labors for himself, for his hungry mouth drives him on" (Prov. 16:26). What is he saying? Does he mean these words literally? Or is he intending to speak in broader terms? While the immediate reference is to food, I believe his intention is to speak of anything material. No matter what they are, material things do not satisfy our souls. There is a sense in which our lives are filled with working so we can eat, and eating so we can find the strength to keep on working. On and on it goes. It is an endless cycle, a vanity.

Obviously, we do not take this sort of verdict without a fight.

Solomon knows his secular opponent is not going to like it either, so he follows his assertion about food with another bold claim.

> For what more has the wise man than the fool?
> What does the poor man have,
> Who knows how to walk before the living? (6:8).

It may be better to have wisdom than folly (see 2:13), but our experience shows us that a wise man does not necessarily have more than a fool. "A fool and his money are soon parted," the old saying goes; but the fact that he had it to lose in the first place proves that even fools do quite well for themselves occasionally! We already have discovered that the wise man's wisdom brings him sorrow (see 2:15–16); he sees the truth about life's vanity clearly, while the fool wallows in his ignorant folly.

The second half of verse 8 asks what the poor man gets for walking an upright life. The answer is the same as for the wise man: nobody really knows. He may be better off, or he may not be. How is the secular mind to know for sure? In either case, both questions point to the next verse.

> Better is the sight of the eyes than the wandering of desire.
> This also is vanity and grasping for the wind (6:9).

Another way of saying this is, "It is better to be content with what you see (see 11:9) than to let your desires wander to what others have (see 4:4). To strive after these things is like chasing the wind." Better to enjoy what we have than to be filled with restlessness or envy over what is not ours. Matthew 6:33 says, "But seek first the kingdom of God and His righteousness." When our first desire is God's kingdom, then He can trust us with our desires.

We should not work for the purpose of material gain. Of course we must work, but we should do so for the glory of God. We need to be content with what God gives us. "We work," Solomon says, "to fill our mouths." "And yet the soul is not satisfied" (v. 7). We have no way of knowing whether our financial goals will bring us satisfaction if we meet them. Judging by Solomon's observations, by themselves they will not.

WHO KNOWS WHETHER WEALTH WILL BE GOOD FOR US?

Solomon concludes his argument in this section of Ecclesiastes with some interesting questions; few people on the road to wealth ever bother to ask them. "When I get it, how do I know it will be good for me? Will it be worth the cost? Maybe down the road I will need patience, and all I will have is a pile of gold at several hundred dollars per ounce. Maybe I will need strength of character, and all I will have is a fortune. Maybe I will need hope instead of money."

> Whatever one is, he has been named already,
> For it is known that he is man;
> And he cannot contend with Him
>   who is mightier than he.
> Since there are many things that increase vanity,
> How is man the better?

> For who knows what is good for man in life, all the days of his vain life which he passes like a shadow? Who can tell a man what will happen after him under the sun? (6:10–12).

God already has a plan; He also knows that we are merely man, nothing more. It is interesting to note that at both 1:9 and 3:15 the same point is made. We cannot alter who we are, and we cannot alter the world God has made. We came from the dust, and we will return to the dust (see Gen. 2:19; 3:19). We are human beings. That is the all-important reality. God has made us in His image, but we still are mortal creatures. Only He is immortal.

"For it is known that he is man; and he cannot contend with Him who is mightier than he" (6:10). It is futile to fight with God. We cannot defeat His plans; He always wins. The letter to the Romans says, "But indeed, O man, who are you to reply against God? Will the thing formed say to him who formed it, 'Why have you made me like this?'" (Rom. 9:20).

When Solomon says that we cannot fight with God, he is warning us not to strive for our own plans. Instead, we should fit into God's plans. Since His plan is perfect in every way, it would be foolish (vain) indeed for us to want to go our own way. His way has to be better than ours. Other ways can only "increase vanity."

The key to this whole section lies in the next verse. "For who knows what is good for man in life, all the days of his vain life which he passes like a shadow?" (6:12). "Our lives pass so quickly," he says. This image is reminiscent of Psalm 102:11, where the psalmist complains that his days are not only like a shadow, but they are like a shadow that lengthens—a short day at that! Solomon concludes, "Who can tell a man what will happen after him under the sun?"

Solomon is not talking about heaven or hell in these verses; he is talking about life "under the sun"—life here and now. We do not know what the future "under the sun" will bring; and since we do not know what is in the future, how do we know whether wealth would be to our advantage? How do we know life would be better?

It is a fair question. At the end of Ecclesiastes Solomon will tell us that the key to everything lies in two truths: "Fear God and keep His commandments" (12:13). For now, though, he is content to raise the question nobody can answer.

We simply do not know what we need. We do not know it now; we will not know it in the future either.

Once again, Solomon's insights have different meanings for those who believe than they do for secular man. These bold statements remind the believer that the present and the future are in good hands. Those who cannot allow room for a loving Father God in this world are caught on the horns of a dilemma. They see the truth of what Solomon says: they have no way of knowing whether they will enjoy the wealth they crave. And they have no way of knowing whether it will be good for them or bad. Until they are ready to trust Solomon's God, they are stuck on those horns.

For the one who believes, there is no such dilemma; there are no horns on which he may be impaled. Instead, there are arms, arms of the loving Father whose every desire is for the best for all His children.

> No good thing will He withhold
> From those who walk uprightly (Ps. 84:11).

CHAPTER TEN

What Value Can There Be in Suffering?

Ecclesiastes 7:1–10

I believe W. C. Fields is the one credited with the remark, "I've been rich and I've been poor. I'd rather be rich." If we were to apply his statement to suffering, we might say, "I've had trouble and I've not had it. I'd rather not have it." We would wonder about the emotional health of someone who preferred suffering and misery to health and happiness.

But is "Thanks, but no thanks!" the only thing we can say about suffering?

I think of Karl Kassulke who played strong safety for the Minnesota Vikings for ten seasons. Karl was known for his reckless lifestyle, both on and off the football field. Then a freak motorcycle accident on a suburban interstate highway ended his career, and he was left with a severed spine and paralysis in most of his body. Suffering? Yes. Tragedy? His own verdict: "Obviously, I didn't think I needed that motorcycle accident. But that was what it took to bring me to my knees. I don't think I ever would have done it otherwise. It was what I needed. It was God's grace to me."*

I think of Joni Eareckson, whose bestselling book, *Joni,* inspired millions and instilled hope in thousands. A beautiful teen-ager, she severed her spinal cord in a diving accident. Helpless, she struggled with her rehabilitation, crying out to God, "How could this happen to me, a believer?" However, as a result of her victory over the pain thrust upon her life, she came to see the goodness of God in everything. God has given her a ministry she never would have known if she had not experienced tragedy.

I think of Diane Bringgold, whose husband and three children were killed in an airplane crash near Mount Shasta in California.

---

*Karl Kassulke and Ron Pitkin, *Kassulke* (Nashville, Tenn.: Thomas Nelson, 1981), p. 219.

Badly burned herself, she tells in her book, *Life Instead,* how in the midst of all her pain and suffering Christ ministered to her. The tragedy she experienced has made it possible for her to minister to others who suffer.

So suffering is not *always* evil! It is not always "vanity." Value can come from it, too.

Jesus understood suffering. He knew its value, and He knew He would suffer. "The Son of Man must suffer many things" (Luke 9:22) was how He faced the suffering He would endure. If He had been unwilling to suffer on our behalf, how different the world would be. None of us would be saved; we would not be reconciled to God. So there was great value in the suffering of Jesus.

Could there be great value in our suffering, for ourselves and for others? Scripture makes it clear; we are called by God to suffer. "For to you it has been granted on behalf of Christ, not only to believe in Him, but also to suffer for His sake" (Phil. 1:29). "Rejoice to the extent that you partake of Christ's sufferings . . . If anyone suffers as a Christian, let him not be ashamed, but let him glorify God in this matter" (1 Pet. 4:13, 16). There is more to suffering than meets the eye.

Solomon has a way of turning the tables on us. While we desire wealth and dislike suffering, he sees them both differently. In chapter six he declares that the value of riches is uncertain and prosperity is not necessarily good. Then in chapter seven he says that adversity, or suffering, is not necessarily evil.

Some plants thrive better in darkness than in light; some qualities grow better in adversity than in ease. This is not always true; some plants wither and die in the darkness, and some people are destroyed by suffering. There is one thing of which we can be sure, though. Sooner or later, suffering will come our way. The question is, will we benefit from it? Or will it destroy us?

The same sun that melts wax hardens clay. The adversity that causes one person to blossom and grow in the Lord destroys another. Unless we have been in situations that try us, we are not likely to grow. However, there is a danger that we might not be strong.

In this section of Ecclesiastes Solomon continues his confrontation with the secular mindset. He says, "Let's take a close look at suffering and affliction. You can't avoid the subject altogether.

Sooner or later, you or someone you love will face suffering. What will it mean? How will you handle it?" Of course, once again it will have very different meanings for those who love and serve the Lord than it will for those who do not.

How does God use adversity for good?

BETTER THAN LAUGHTER

Better is an important word in Ecclesiastes. It is used 23 times throughout the book, but nowhere more regularly than here (four times in four verses), and certainly nowhere in a more striking way. It is as if Solomon says, "Let your sorrow make you better, not bitter."

> A good name is better than precious ointment,
> And the day of death than the day of one's birth.
> It is better to go to the house of mourning
> Than to go to the house of feasting,
> For that is the end of all men;
> And the living will take it to heart.
> Sorrow is better than laughter,
> For by a sad countenance the heart is made better.
> The heart of the wise is in the house of mourning,
> But the heart of fools is in the house of mirth (7:1–4).

In Proverbs 17:22 Solomon wrote, "A merry heart does good, like medicine,/But a broken spirit dries the bones." So he is not speaking against laughter or happiness as a matter of principle. He must have had another point in mind.

If Solomon intended to shock his audience with verse 1, he certainly must have been pleased with its results. The assertion that the day of one's death is better than the day of one's birth comes at us with no warning. Certainly, he was not referring to life after death, as the apostle Paul was when he wrote of "having a desire to depart and be with Christ, which is far better" (Phil. 1:23). The subject here is life, here and now.

Solomon is comparing two days—the day of birth and the day of death. His comparison, "A good name is better than precious ointment;" is parallel to "the day of death [is better] than the day of one's birth" (7:1). Precious ointment was a perfume used on happy occasions, as on the day of a birth. It was precious, but not as precious as a good name. You can buy the ointment; a good name cannot be purchased for any price. So some things are definitely better than others. But how can the day of death be better than the day of life?

The answer is in verse 2: "It is better to go to the house of mourning than to go to the house of feasting, for that is the end of all men; and the living will take it to heart" (7:2). We learn more through death than through birth. None of us learned much at our birth. We do not learn much at the birth of someone else, either. It is a day for rejoicing, not for reflecting on the somber reality of death or the meaning of life. It is a happy time, but we learn very little of ultimate value at a celebration. There is so much, though, to learn at the time of death!

The psalmist wrote, "So teach us to number our days,/That we may gain a heart of wisdom" (Ps. 90:12). The day of death is a day when we number our days. We look at our lives and take stock; we become fertile soil for the growth of God's Word.

I thought of that recently at the funeral of a dear, beloved member of our church. She loved the Lord and walked with Him for seventy-five years. She knew how to live with gusto; and when the time came, she knew how to die with beauty. As I looked around the congregation, I saw several people whom she had touched for God. I also remembered how she had been a teacher and helper in the Sunday school for over fifty years. At her funeral I thought of many things—the brevity of life, the value of serving the Lord, the joy of being with Him in glory someday. It was a "better" day for me; once again I was able to take the reality of life, the truth, to my heart. Eventually my own turn will come.

Solomon also said that sorrow has a refining influence on us. "Sorrow is better than laughter, for by a sad countenance the heart is made better. The heart of the wise is in the house of mourning, but the heart of fools is in the house of mirth" (7:3–4). He does not say that we should have sorrow instead of laughter; it is merely "better." There is a value system at work here—good, better, and best. Through sorrow our hearts are made better. Indeed, sorrow can be the bedrock upon which the truest form of joy can be built.

Again, Solomon's words will have different meanings to the believer and the unbeliever. To the unbeliever, the only reason to take note of death is to be sure not to let any of life's gusto slip through his fingers. If this life is all there is, then he had better gather flowers while they bloom. Solomon acknowledges this in verse 4, "The heart of fools is in the house of mirth." The fool wants to repress all thought of the inevitability of death.

The Christian, though, sees a very different message in Solomon's wisdom, as the believing Jew of Solomon's day would have seen. In tough times our hearts are softened and made pliable in God's hands. Through grief and sorrow, God can do the kind of work in us that will make us glad, if we will allow Him the freedom to work. "Now no chastening seems to be joyful for the present, but grievous; nevertheless, afterward it yields the peaceable fruit of righteousness to those who have been trained by it" (Heb. 12:11).

Solomon's father, David, wrote, "Before I was afflicted, I went astray,/But now I keep Your word. . . . It is good for me that I have been afflicted,/That I may learn Your statutes" (Ps. 119:67, 71). The apostle Paul wrote, "We also glory in tribulations, knowing that tribulation produces perseverance" (Rom. 5:3). Again, the advice of Scripture is:

> When all kinds of trials and temptations crowd into your lives, my brothers, don't resent them as intruders, but welcome them as friends! Realise that they come to test your faith and to produce in you the quality of endurance. But let the process go on until that endurance is fully developed, and you will find you have become men of mature character, men of integrity, with no weak spots (James 1:2–4, PHILLIPS).

God does not waste sorrow or adversity. Malachi 3:3 says, "He [God] will sit as a refiner and a purifier of silver." He knows the purpose for which we go through tragedy and sorrow. It is for our good, and the good of His kingdom.

BETTER THAN PRAISE

Certainly, it is easier to receive praise than rebuke; praise is also easier to give. The wise person will carefully listen to the rebukes he receives. Frequently they contain a great deal more love than praise does.

It is better to hear the rebuke of the wise
Than for a man to hear the song of fools (7:5).

It is better to be rebuked by a wise man than to be complimented by a fool.

None of us really likes to be told we made a mistake. When someone tells us we did a poor job at something, we may easily become discouraged. When someone tries to show us how to do something better, we may become offended, especially if we believe it to be an area in which we are particularly strong. None of us enjoys being corrected. We would rather have just about anyone say, "You are absolutely the greatest thing in the world. You do everything well." We know it is not true, but we like it anyway and are sure God will forgive the person for lying (and us for enjoying it)!

In another place Solomon wrote, "Faithful are the wounds of a friend;/But the kisses of an enemy are deceitful" (Prov. 27:6). I have learned some of the most important lessons of my life when a friend cared enough for me to risk our friendship and tell me what I needed to know. I do not recall ever liking to hear it, even if I smiled while the words were being said. Not once! But when I have been willing to swallow my pride and get on my knees before God, I've learned my most important lessons. "Faithful are the wounds of a friend." Indeed!

If we are unwilling to be rebuked or corrected, we will go through life unaware of much of what God wants for us; for God often corrects us through others. Husbands, wives, and children ought to think about this. Who on the face of all the earth loves us more than our spouse or our parents? Whose advice should we be able to trust more? I can think of no one's.

THE LAUGHTER OF THE FOOL

There is humor in verse 6:

For like the crackling of thorns
    under a pot,
So is the laughter of the fool.
This also is vanity (7:6).

When I light my fireplace on a cold winter night, I have a choice. I can either hold my match under a pile of kindling or under a large log. If I go the kindling route, the match will quickly cause a fire. If I try to light the log, nothing happens. However, if I have a fire made of logs, it will burn for hours; but if I am content to use twigs and kindling only, my fire will either flame fast and burn out quickly or I will have to continue feeding it every few minutes.

So it is with a fire made of crackling thorns. There is little to it. Oh, it is a noisy fire, much like the laughter of the fool is filled with much noise. The irony is that at first it appears as if it is a better fire than the one made correctly, but the truth quickly becomes apparent. There is much noise and light, and it spreads its warmth quickly. But its heat is negligible because it comes and goes in a few seconds. So is the praise of fools. It is "vain," empty and without substance. The praise of fools is of no more value than the heat of a pile of thorns is for cooking food.

BETTER THAN FRETTING

I was preparing to preach on the subject, "Love is patient" from 1 Corinthians 13:4 (rsv). I decided to take a break and pick up a new part for my son's stereo. As I was driving to the store, I heard a siren to my right and saw an ambulance rapidly approaching me on the access ramp to the highway. I would have to slow my speed quickly, or else I would hit the ambulance. Needless to say, the man following me crashed into the rear of my nearly new car!

After I called the police to report the accident, it seemed (to this preacher who was in the midst of preparing a sermon on patience!) as if they took forever to arrive. Once I was finished with them, I decided to get an estimate for the repair to my car and called ahead so I would not have to wait long. Anyone who ever has been in a rush knows the rest of the story! Delay followed delay, with my frustration growing by the minute. Finally, the Lord had to remind me of my sermon: Love is patient. It is patient not just with those we know well, but also with strangers who are having a bad day and are delaying ours.

Patience *is* better than fretting!

The end of a thing is better than its beginning,
And the patient in spirit is better than the proud in spirit.
Do not hasten in your spirit to be angry,
For anger rests in the bosom of fools.
Do not say, "Why were the former days better than these?"
For you do not inquire wisely concerning this (7:8–10).

There is much wisdom in these verses. The problems Solomon discusses in them—worry, impatience, pride, anger, romanticizing the past—seem to plague each generation. Why does he talk about them here? And why does he bring them together the way he does?

Remember that Solomon is talking about what is better. Often adversity or suffering is better than laughter; we learn more from it. Often correction is better than flattery or praise; we learn from it, too. Now Solomon moves on to these immature ways in which we indulge ourselves and which only serve to defeat us. For the Christian, they serve to remind us of the fact that our days are in God's hands; they simply remind the nonbeliever that each of these actions is foolish. Pragmatically speaking, they are self-destructive; they are vain.

When he says, "The end of a thing is better than its beginning," Solomon is warning us to look at the big picture, not the smallness of beginnings or the setbacks we incur along the way. We need to keep the apostle Paul's viewpoint in mind: "I press toward the goal . . ." (Phil. 3:14). We should be patient; we should not be deterred or discouraged along the way. If God is in something, then we know it will be successful according to His purpose for it. We can rest in that.

Furthermore, patience is important. "And the patient in spirit is better than the proud in spirit" (v. 8). Patience and pride are opposites; a proud person is seldom a patient one. The proud person is self-centered. Because he is concerned with himself, he is not patient with others. "Love is patient" (1 Cor 13:4 RSV). When we truly love others, we will try to meet their needs. We will be patient with them. But if our primary interest is in getting what *we* want from life, we will be impatient with others. So self-centeredness and impatience go together, as do humility and patience.

How does the fool handle the frustrations of life? Solomon tells us: "Do not hasten in your spirit to be angry, for anger rests in the bosom of fools" (7:9). The fool's approach to his problems is anger. He generates more heat than light. Even on a merely pragmatic, secular basis the fool's response makes no sense! When he is angry, he loses his ability to think clearly and gets himself in even worse trouble.

This is a place where we believers must apply our theology. We know that God is going to accomplish His purposes on earth. We know the results of history in advance—God wins! So if I am a child of His, I can say: "I know I am His child and will share in His victory. Therefore, I can see through all the suffering and sorrow and adversity. And rather than being impatient or angry with life, I can look forward in faith to the day when God will bring in His kingdom."

Solomon cuts through the futility of worrying with the words, "Do not say, 'Why were the former days better than these?'" (7:10). Nowhere does the folly of our impatience show through better than here. The person who laments the passing of the "good old days" does not remember them very well. I would not trade today for those days for anything. These are the days God has given me! And furthermore, I like life today.

People long for the past for several reasons. The first is a poor memory (perhaps it would be better to call it a creative memory!). The second reason is that it is easier to escape from today's realities through nostalgia than it is to find ways to handle today's problems. We find it uncomfortable to live with the things we see around us, and we long for a more familiar day (and more familiar problems, I might add!). Third, it is easier to complain than to deal with problems constructively. If we take responsibility for today, we are making a commitment to work for a better world. It is easier to complain. Fourth, it is often a childish, immature way of expressing disappointment. It is much like the child who decides to take his ball and go home when the game does not go his way. Rather than hang in there and grow, we retreat and wither.

Solomon knew all this; and he declares, "For you do not inquire wisely concerning this" (7:10). We are fools when we long for a previous "golden age," as foolish as Ponce de León was when he sought the fountain of youth. One era is basically like all others (see 1:9–10).

It is easy for Christians today to be discouraged. Immorality is flaunted on every side. An abortion is as easy to get as a new set of tires. Business leaders corrupt politicians, and corrupted politicians seek even larger bribes. In far too many homes family life has degenerated into a quarrelsome battleground. The threat of nuclear war becomes more ominous every year, and the political leaders of many lands seem to go out of their way to look for conflict.

Yet, in the face of these discouraging realities, we need to remember the One who will have the last word. One day the blast of God's trumpet will ring forth from heaven, and God's new age will begin.

Whatever our fears, or whatever uncertainties we must learn to accept, we must not cry, "Why were the former days better than these?" They never were. But even more important, the end—the completion—of God's work is even better than its beginning.

Vince Lombardi was right. Winning isn't the most important thing. It's the only thing. Through Christ we have been made winners!

So what is there to fear?

CHAPTER ELEVEN
The Excellence of Wisdom

Ecclesiastes 7:11–29

During a recent summer, my wife drove north one morning with our daughter to visit her parents for several days. Our son was in Africa on a short-term missionary project, and I was left alone to take care of the house—and myself. As the week came to a close, I noticed that I was beginning to run out of dishes. Dirty dishes seemed to be stacked everywhere.

Sunday morning came, and I still had not gotten around to cleaning up the kitchen; so in the afternoon I realized that if I wanted them clean before Dee came home, I would have to do them before I left for the evening service at church. I would be driving north myself to meet Dee and Kristen immediately following the service. As I was working at it, the tornado sirens began to wail. Since tornadoes are a fairly common occurrence in Minnesota, I was not all that concerned.

As busy as I was, I more or less ignored the sirens, until I realized that they were on for a reason and I was foolish to pay no attention to them. The least I could do was turn on the television for information about where the funnels had been sighted. As I washed and listened, I realized that my home was directly in the path of one of the funnels. I was supposed to go to the basement immediately and lie under a table or something sturdy for protection.

But I did not have time for that!

I had to make a decision, and I did. I knew I was ready to meet the Lord, but I was not sure I was ready to meet my wife with a house full of dirty dishes. So I kept on washing.

We are constantly making decisions. Sometimes we make right ones, and other times we make wrong ones. The person who wants to serve the Lord desires to know God's will and obey Him more than anything else, but many other factors get in the way. We are bombarded with all sorts of temptations to compromise or confuse us—greed, lust, envy, fear, pride, self-love. Our culture preaches consumerism and hedonism, both boldly and subtly. If ever God's people needed wisdom for the living of their lives, it is today.

There are far too many distractions that would blur our vision and make it difficult to know the difference between right and wrong. We need the wisdom of God.

In another book Solomon declared, "The beginning of wisdom is this: Get wisdom, and whatever you get, get insight" (Prov. 4:7 RSV). In another chapter of that book he wrote, "The fear of the LORD is the beginning of knowledge" (1:7). In other words, if you want to get wisdom, get on with it! Begin by fearing God.

What does it mean to fear God? Certainly it includes an element of being afraid of God; after all, He is the Almighty! Anyone who is not following God's will should fear Him. But the fear of the Lord includes much more; it includes one's whole relationship with God. We are to reverence Him, to honor Him, to worship and adore Him—with all that we are. That is what it means to fear the Lord. We may have worldly knowledge about Him without reverencing or honoring or worshiping Him. However, while we live in that state, we will not have wisdom. We will not see life as God sees it, and we will not know what He expects of us.

Wisdom is desirable. It is to be sought. Throughout Ecclesiastes, Solomon refers both to it (chapters 1, 2, 7, 8, 9, 10) and to the wise (chapters 2, 4, 6, 7, 8, 9, 10, 12). Wisdom is one of Solomon's primary concerns as he writes this book, and nowhere does he examine it more closely than in these verses. What is it that makes wisdom such an excellent way in which to walk? Why is it that we are to pursue it? What gain is there in it?

WISDOM IS A PROTECTION

When I look back on the mistakes I have made and the sins I have committed, I am amazed that they always have come from not living within the wisdom of God. Solomon experienced that, too. He knew there was a protection in God's wisdom, and he knew we can only enjoy that protection when we obey God.

Wisdom is good with an inheritance,
And profitable to those who see the sun.

> For wisdom is a defense as money is a defense,
> But the excellence of knowledge is that wisdom gives life to those
>   who have it.
> Consider the work of God;
> For who can make straight what He has made crooked?
> In the day of prosperity be joyful,
> But in the day of adversity consider:
> Surely God has appointed the one as well as the other,
> So that man can find nothing that will happen after him (7:11–14).

Solomon seems to be thinking of wisdom in terms of its utility, the gain it brings us. This is quite unlike his comments in Proverbs where he declares wisdom to be priceless: "For wisdom is better than rubies,/And all the things one may desire cannot be compared with her" (8:11). In practical terms, even if we were to inherit vast wealth, we would still need wisdom to protect us from our foolishness (see 7:11). Furthermore, wisdom will be "profitable" only to the living, "to those who see the sun" (7:11). We must obtain its benefits now; wisdom will do us no good once we are dead.

Another translation of verse 12 reads:

> For the protection of wisdom is like
>   the protection of money;
> and the advantage of knowledge
>   is that wisdom preserves the life
>   of him who has it (7:12 RSV).

The idea that wisdom is protection is an important theme of Solomon's writing.

In light of this it is refreshing to note Solomon's comments concerning wisdom: "She is a tree of life to those who take hold of her" (Prov. 3:18). "For whoever finds me [wisdom] finds life,/And obtains favor from the LORD" (Prov. 8:35). Wisdom is life-giving in the sense that whoever finds it is in touch with the life of God.

It is important to remember the historical situation when Solomon penned these words. Israel was experiencing success and wealth unlike anything it had ever known, but it had begun to deteriorate from within, first in its leadership and then throughout the nation. Because of its wealth, Israel was able to buy some protection through alliances. The people understand the power that wealth brings; Solomon knew it was also important for them to realize that wisdom is superior to wealth. Its "advantage" is that it "preserves the life of him who has it" (7:12 RSV). This is true on a national level when nations try to use their wealth and power to control events to their advantage and on the personal level when individuals seek to buy the esteem of others. It is "better" to follow the Lord and seek His wisdom. The protection that wealth purchases is always for sale to the highest bidder, and it is of no comfort to one who ignores God.

Earlier in Ecclesiastes Solomon has written, "What is crooked cannot be made straight, and what is lacking cannot be numbered" (1:15). That is, it does no good to wish we could change those things over which we have no control.

Verse 13 reminds us once again of the crooked things. They are crooked from our vantage point; we see them as being to our disadvantage. For the one who leaves God out of the picture, this verdict is a discouragement; for the believer, however, it is a reminder of God's sovereignty. God loves the world; He loves us; His activities are always good.

All of us have "crooked" places—physical appearance, relatives, job, economic situation, health—whatever. A believer can accept them, knowing that the sovereign God knows best. This is not a call to stoic passivity, as if we are to accept everything about life without thinking. We ought to change those things God leads us to change. We ought to make the wrong things right, insofar as we can. But there are "crooked" things we cannot straighten, and we must learn to believe and say: "God, You are God. You are good and powerful. I trust You. I believe in You. And even though I don't like some of these things that come from Your hand, by faith I accept them with joy."

The only thing that can keep us from affirming these "crooked" things as blessings from the Lord is a temporal, secular value system. A secular value system will keep us from believing that in His goodness God has made some crooked things that we cannot straighten. It says: "I am only concerned about right now; the future isn't important. I'm more concerned about my comfort and convenience than I am about godliness and being available to the Lord." A secular value system has no room for a sovereign God (other than self). Consequently, when we realize that the earth is

God's and He is its Lord, the secular viewpoint is seen for the foolishness it is. It offers no gain.

We are to be joyful in "the day of prosperity" and in "the day of adversity" (v. 14). God made both of them. Our inclination is to accept "prosperity" and reject "adversity." When Solomon attributes God's motives as being "that man can find nothing that will happen after him" (v. 14), he is aware that we need to trust God—period. If we *knew* what the future was going to bring, we would be even more inclined to do whatever comes to mind. "After all," we might say, "if this is what will happen for sure, it makes no difference what I do." However, if we are dependent on God at each step of the way, we must pay attention as each step is taken. We must trust Him every day.

Some time ago Grant Howard, a professor at Western Seminary in Portland, Oregon, spoke in our church. He used this same text. He told us how one day he felt so prosperous. Life was going great. He was on top of the world. He told of attending a track meet.

> I was at Arcadia High School in Phoenix, Arizona, watching my son Jim throw the discus in a track meet. He was throwing well and when the competition was over and the measurements were made, he came running over to me with the news that he had not only won but had broken the school record. As a freshman he had thrown the discus farther than any freshman before him. For his father this was a moment of prosperity! I was happy! All that talent packed into one boy! He undoubtedly had inherited it from his father! I was leaning against the fence indulging in this moment of immense prosperity when my wife and three other children arrived. I informed them of Jim's achievements and they rejoiced with me. But then my wife, Audrey, brought her news into the arena. "Dr. Mattson just called about the pathology report on the mole you had removed this week. You've got cancer." (*Knowing God's Will and Doing It* (Zondervan, 1976), p. 57).

Dr. Howard's comment was, "That was adversity. And God made the one as surely as He made the other."

As crooked as it seems, he was right.

It is important to believe the truth in that statement. We must allow God to be large enough that we can trust Him in the day of prosperity and not let that prosperity turn us from the course. It is equally important that we let Him be large enough that our faith is not damaged or destroyed in the day of adversity. God has His purposes for both.

The wisdom of God protects us. If we live in it, we trust Him in both straight and crooked places, joy and sorrow, success or failure. Wisdom says, "Trust Him. He knows more than you do. He cares about you." "He who did not spare His own Son, but delivered Him up for us all, how shall He not with Him also freely give us all things?" (Rom. 8:32).

What protection there is in that!

WISDOM IS A STRENGTH

Wisdom is more than protection; it is also strength.

> I have seen all things in my days of vanity:
> There is a just man who perishes in his righteousness,
> And there is a wicked man who prolongs his life in his wickedness.
> Do not be overly righteous,
> Nor be overly wise:
> Why should you destroy yourself?
> Do not be overly wicked,
> Nor be foolish:
> Why should you die before your time?
> It is good that you grasp this,
> And also not remove your hand from the other;
> For he who fears God will escape them all.
> Wisdom strengthens the wise
> More than ten rulers of the city (7:15–19).

Once again Solomon picks up on the secularist's attitude toward wisdom. "What good is it?" he might ask. "When good men die and wicked men prosper, what is the point of living by wisdom?" From his point of view, the secularist makes sense. If faith is unknown or ignored, there seems to be no purpose in wisdom.

Furthermore, the advice not to be overly righteous, wise, or wicked sounds very sensible to the secularist. The Chinese are reported to have a saying, "The shoot that grows tall is the first to be cut." It expresses much the same thought as we find in verses 15 through 18. Solomon's point in including these words is to show that this is the logical conclusion of secular man's life, if he only accepts what he knows with his senses as the only reality.

But the secularist's mindset is not the only thing at work in these verses. "Wisdom strengthens the wise more than ten rulers of the city" (7:19). I believe that Solomon is saying: "Yes, you are right— from your limited vantage point. If you rule out a loving, sovereign God to begin with, it does make a lot of sense to avoid being too good or too evil. You will want to keep your options open. There may be times when it will be to your advantage to be evil, just as it is to be good. However, if all this talk about God *is* true, then wisdom will strengthen you more than many wise rulers will strengthen a city."

A Christian will see through this argument quite quickly. Obviously, Solomon does not mean the words *righteous* or *wicked* in their absolute senses. Only God is absolutely holy or righteous; it is ludicrous to talk of a "righteous" person, just as it is absurd to talk of a "wicked" person, as if we were not all sinners. (Of course, the Christian knows that everyone who is in Christ is made righteous and holy [see Rom. 3:22, 26; 4:11].) Jesus once said, "I have not come to call the righteous, but sinners, to repentance" (Luke 5:32). He also said, "Unless your righteousness exceeds the righteousness of the scribes and Pharisees, you will by no means enter the kingdom of heaven" (Matt. 5:20). In another place the New Testament reads, "But as He who called you is holy, you also be holy in all your conduct, because it is written, 'Be holy, for I am holy'" (1 Pet. 1:15–16). Only God is holy and righteous. We try to appear as if we are, but not one of us is.

But the person who follows in God's way experiences a different reality. His wisdom brings success. His path gets there! God's ways protect him from errors and excesses. The One who made us knows what is best for us. That is why we must seek the wisdom that only comes from God. It is our strength in the midst of a world that has lost its reason for living.

WISDOM IS SCARCE

Having declared the protection and strength of wisdom, Solomon looks around himself and says, "There aren't many wise people." He begins with the cause of this condition.

> For there is not a just man on earth who does good
> And does not sin (7:20).

"For there is not a just man on earth" reminds us of Romans chapter 3:

> There is none righteous, no, not one;
> There is none who understands;
> There is none who seeks after God.
> They have all gone out of the way;
> They have together become unprofitable;
> There is none who does good, no, not one (Rom. 3:10–12).

When Solomon says "there is not a just man on earth," he is stating a fact, not offering an excuse. Indeed, he is declaring his own faith.

In the previous section he argued the case of the secularist to show that wisdom provides more strength than human knowledge. The way of the secularist leads to defeat and weakness; the way of wisdom leads to victory and strength. Here, however, he argues from the position of faith in God and reminds us of a basic Scripture truth: the problem with mankind is sin. This is the basis for every word he utters; it is the reason so few people are wise. They are bound up in their unrighteousness, their sin.

This sin problem expresses itself in our relationships with others (see Romans chapters 1–3 for a full analysis of this problem). Later in chapter seven Solomon will deal with the alienation between the sexes, but first he uses an illustration from work, the master and the servant. We might speak of it as the employer and the employee.

> Also do not take to heart everything people say,
> Lest you hear your servant cursing you.
> For many times, also, your own heart has known
> That even you have cursed others (7:21–22).

Here Solomon is referring to destructive, not constructive, criticism. And who of us has not been stung by adverse criticism? Solomon says we ought to take it with a grain of salt. If there is something to be learned from criticism, then be thankful for it. But if we hear censure that is unfair, we should not become upset.

After all, what difference does it make if it is unfair? We have been unkind and unfair toward others ourselves!

I will never forget an incident from my college days. I was on the second floor of a building on the old campus at Bethel College. A friend of mine was taking apart one of our professors in superlatives, when who should walk around the corner but the very man he was slandering. His name had just been spoken, and we knew he heard it. It was a very low moment for both of us. To my professor's credit, he was gracious. I was not the one saying the bitter things, but I was doing the listening! The lesson was not wasted.

Adverse criticism. What is more destructive? The old story is told of a note being found in the suicide victim's pocket, simply reading, "They said." All of us receive some criticism. We are best off when we overlook it.

Solomon gives us a dismal verdict:

All this I have proved by wisdom.
I said, "I will be wise";
But it was far from me.
As for that which is far off and exceedingly deep,
Who can find it out? (7:23–24).

There is a sense, of course, in which those who have walked with God a long time have gained much wisdom; but that does not seem to be what Solomon is driving at here. Rather, he seems to be saying that—after his elaborate search for wisdom in such things as pleasure, achievement, entertainment, hard work, self-fulfillment, and all the mundane experiences of life—he failed to find wisdom. He could even be expressing the thoughts of secular man for him after he, too, has carefully thought through each of the areas Solomon has explored.

His verdict: "It was far from me. . . . who can find it out?" is the cry of every person who has sought the meaning of life apart from God. It cannot be found there.

So he turns to relationships; but they, like everything else, are marred by sin.

I applied my heart to know,
To search and seek out wisdom and the reason of things,
To know the wickedness of folly,

Even of foolishess and madness.
And I find more bitter than death
The woman whose heart is snares and nets,
Whose hands are fetters,
He who pleases God shall escape from her,
But the sinner shall be taken by her.
"Here is what I have found," says the Preacher,
"Adding one thing to the other to find out the reason,
Which my soul still seeks but I cannot find:
One man among a thousand I have found,
But a woman among all these I have not found" (7:25–28).

When Solomon speaks of "the wickedness of folly," he is saying that nothing is more stupid than folly, or sin. It is foolishness; it is madness. He applies his lesson to the adulterous woman, a subject of which it seems reasonable to assume Solomon had intimate knowledge (in view of his thousand wives and concubines, see 1 Kings 11:3). The sin he describes in verse 26 cheapens and distorts even the closest and most intimate relationship with which God blessed mankind (see Gen. 2:24).

There is no point in documenting the rampant immorality of our time; it is all too apparent. It is also apparent, however, that even Christians find themselves wondering if perhaps the biblical commands against fornication and adultery are outmoded. Solomon's own life was certainly a disaster at this point. However, his experience also gave him ample reason to reflect on the meaning of his sin, and God used him to pen some of the Scriptures' most vivid warnings about the dangers of fornication and adultery.

In Proverbs Solomon wrote that if you follow wisdom, you will be saved from immorality.

When wisdom enters your heart,
And knowledge is pleasant to your soul,
Discretion will preserve you;
Understanding will keep you . . . .
To deliver you from the immoral woman,
From the seductress who flatters with her words,
Who forsakes the companion of her youth,
And forgets the covenant of her God.
For her house leads down to death,
And her paths to the dead;

None who go to her return,
Nor do they regain the paths of life (2:10–11, 16–19).

Is immorality serious or not? "None who go to her return, nor do
they regain the paths of life." It is not that God will not forgive
sexual sin; He does and will. But this sin marks us in a way no other
sin does, and we never quite get over it. The longer I have pastored
and the more people with whom I have counseled, the more I see
the truth of Solomon's verdict worked out in human experience.

Wisdom will keep us from immorality. If we fail, God's forgiveness will cleanse us from the guilt of sin once we confess it and
repent. Solomon speaks so strongly against this sin because he
knew its devastating impact personally. We should not take his
words lightly.

Solomon could have done much better himself in this area. In
one sense, we might be snide and suggest, "If he couldn't find a
good woman, it wasn't from lack of trying!" To do that, however,
would be to distort the text. Granted, for a wise man he was surely
a fool where women were concerned. And granted, his view of
women must have been terribly warped. While he could pass judgment on a thousand women, a thousand women could deliver the
same verdict on him!

I have yet to find a commentator who offers a completely satis-
factory explanation as to why Solomon said that he was able to find
one man among a thousand, but not one woman. Surely he was
aware of the stories of the godly judge Deborah (see Judg. 4–5) and
of Samuel's godly mother Hannah (see 1 Sam. 1–2). It seems too
simple to merely pass him off as a male chauvinist; for in Proverbs
12:4; 14:1; 18:22, and 19:14 he speaks very highly of women in
general.

Perhaps the clue to this question is to be found by regarding the
phrase "one man among a thousand" as a Hebrew equivalent to our
"one in a million." If this is the case, his comment about women
could be an equally idiomatic way of speaking of women and we
have not yet learned enough about the language and culture to
decipher his exact meaning. Frankly, there is not much difference
between one in a thousand and none!

Regardless, it is obvious what the punch line of Solomon's comment is in verse 29:

Truly, this only I have found:
That God made man upright,
But they have sought out many schemes (7:29).

Granted, wisdom is rare in a man (or in a woman). Why? Men
are sinners (see 7:20) and "have sought out many schemes" even
though God made them upright. Later, Isaiah would pen the same
sentiments in another period of Israel's history: "All we like sheep
have gone astray;/We have turned, everyone, to his own way" (Is.
53:6). Isaiah went on to speak of the grace of God in the second half
of the verse, "And the Lord has laid on Him [Jesus] the iniquity of
us all."

Solomon does not talk of a Deliverer in these verses, but his
picture of humanity certainly demands one. Instead, he points us
to the beginning: "God made man upright" (v. 29). Once we know
that, we can see that our folly is our own doing. We are at fault. We
are accountable. But by telling us that God made us upright—
morally straight—in the beginning, Solomon reminds us that
there is more to life than the vanities the Book of Ecclesiastes so
eloquently proclaims.

CHAPTER TWELVE
When Our Vision Isn't 20/20

Ecclesiastes 8:1–17

I know of no one who better illustrates mankind's distorted vision than the cartoon character of television fame, Mr. Magoo. Magoo has the uncanny misfortune of completely misinterpreting every situation he encounters. His circumstances are frequently ludicrous, and sometimes potentially disastrous; but somehow Mr. Magoo keeps on muddling and stumbling through life, much like the kitten whose eyes have not yet opened to the world.

I find it easy to identify with Mr. Magoo; sometimes my vision is blinded by circumstances. But Mr. Magoo has a broader symbolic meaning than any one person's experiences; he is a parable of mankind. Granted, few people ever encounter the comic situations in which he frequently is placed, but all of us do have great difficulty "seeing" things as they really are. Our vision is limited. We can only see for short distances, and we are limited by time.

Throughout Ecclesiastes, Solomon has repeatedly asked us to look at life very carefully, to see it for what it is. As a result, we have explored many areas with him—wisdom, pleasure, fulfillment, good, evil, work, friendship, wealth. In the process we have discovered that everything about life has a different meaning for those who have faith in God than it does for those who live a secular lifestyle.

If we take the secularist at his word and look at the world only in terms of what we can see, touch, taste, and smell (empiricism), we will be led to despair. We cannot count on the things we love or possess; they can be taken away from us. And even if no one ever takes them from us, ultimately death will take us from them. Since that is the sum total of life "under the sun," it is a pretty devastating verdict for secular man to face.

Life looks very different to the believer. Since he knows that life continues into eternity, he is not threatened by death. Rather, death is seen as merely one experience in life among many. And since the believer trusts in an infinite, personal, and loving God, death can take away nothing important. This God we love loves us unconditionally, and He can be trusted.

At this point in his argument, Solomon takes a slightly modified course; he reminds those of us who love and serve the Lord that our vision is not 20/20 either. There are realities of life that defy our understanding, no matter how intelligent we are or how sincere our faith is.

The truth, of course, is that our vision never has been 20/20. Verse 29 of chapter 7 has reminded us of that already: "Truly, this only I have found:/That God made men upright,/But they have sought out many schemes." Our "schemes" have distorted our vision, and Solomon asks us to consider what our limited vision means when we face the uncomfortable, inscrutable realities of life.

WHEN OUR LEADERS ABUSE US

It is significant that when Solomon begins to discuss our relationship to rulers, he begins with a word of caution. Whether we face the capricious tyranny that frequently exists under a king (as was the case in the biblical world) or a dictator (which is more common in our own time) or whether we must deal with the powerful vested interests in our own democratic society, it is wise to be discreet when dealing with anyone who has real authority over us. Listen to Solomon's advice:

Who is like a wise man?
And who knows the interpretation of a thing?
A man's wisdom makes his face shine,
And the sternness of his face is changed.

I counsel you, "Keep the king's commandment for the sake of your oath to God. Do not be hasty to go from his presence. Do not take your stand for an evil thing, for he does whatever pleases him." Where the word of a king is, there is power;
And who may say to him, "What are you doing?" (8:1–4).

Who of us really knows enough to know *exactly* what God is doing in our time? And who of us knows enough to know what our own rulers are planning? No one.

We have our opinions, and we probably would prefer to hear some things, rather than others, from our leaders. However, none of us knows what is in the hearts of men—much less God—and none of us knows what the future will bring.

Solomon speaks of the wise man's face shining (see v. 1). There is something to be learned from this expression. Solomon is not telling us to be wise and fake it; he is saying that we should be joyful, no matter what the circumstances are. We are to be a blessing, not a curse. Repeatedly, the writers of Scripture use the image of a shining face to speak of blessing. In the Book of Numbers we read, "The LORD bless you and keep you; the LORD make His face shine upon you, and be gracious to you" (6:24–25). The Psalms repeatedly refer to the Lord's face "shining" upon His people (31:16; 67:1; 80:3, 7, 19; 119:135).

Also, they speak of God's being the source of our blessing: "They looked to Him and were radiant" (Ps. 34:5). When His face shines on us, we are blessed. When our faces shine on the world, we bless it. That it is how we are to *begin* to deal with those in authority over us. We are to be a blessing unto them, even when they are insensitive or cruel.

We are not asked to give up our beliefs, though. We are asked to deal with adversity in the same Spirit as Jesus did when He prayed from the cross, "Father, forgive them . . ." (Luke 23:34). When peace and joy and praise rule in our hearts, they will show through in every circumstance, not just in those we select for ourselves.

A wise person will realize that more is going on in this world than meets the eye. God is in control. He will raise up leaders and rulers, and He will cast down those who oppress His people—in His own good time (see Ps. 2). Rather than walk around with a stern, sad, "cursing" face, it is better to bless those who have authority over us.

Solomon's words at this point are very practical. We instinctively know he is right when he cautions us to obey the king or the ruler. Who has the power to question his actions and get away with it? Instead we are to be discreet and know that those in authority—be they our boss, the government, or whatever—have the power to enforce their demands, whether we like it or not.

This is not the whole picture; it is only the beginning. There is an accounting to be made for the way power is used, and Solomon speaks about it quite forthrightly.

He who keeps his command will experience nothing harmful;
And a wise man's heart discerns both time and judgment,
Because for every matter there is a time and judgment,
Though the misery of man increases greatly.
For he does not know what will happen;
So who can tell him when it will occur?
No one has power over the spirit to retain the spirit,
And no one has power in the day of death.
There is no discharge in that war,
And wickedness will not deliver those who are given to it.

All this I have seen, and applied my heart to every work that is done under the sun: there is a time in which one man rules over another to his own hurt (8:5–9).

Solomon uses subtle irony when he declares that "a wise man's heart discerns both time and judgment" (v. 5). A ruler who is wise will know there is a day of reckoning (a foolish ruler will not) and so will a wise servant (or citizen or employee). For everything there is a time and a reckoning (judgment). "To everything there is a season" (3:1).

Obviously, there are limits to how far a believer can bend in obeying a ruler's commands. We have several illustrations in the Bible, probably none more vivid than those of Daniel and Peter, of people who resisted when they were pushed too far. Daniel, a young Jewish captive who had been taken to Babylon, was ordered to stop praying to God and to worship the king. He refused and was thrown into a den of lions to be killed (see Dan. 6).

When the apostle Peter was ordered by the rulers in Jerusalem to stop preaching about Jesus, he refused to obey them and declared, "We ought to obey God rather than men" (Acts 5:29). When the edicts of rulers or of the government or of our employers interfere with our relationship with God, we disobey them to obey God.

Certainly, our circumstances vary greatly from those Daniel and Peter experienced, and we must examine our motives and circumstances very carefully before standing against our leaders. But the principle is a scriptural one, and we ignore it to our own detriment.

Paul's letter to the Romans provides an important balance to this principle. It reminds us that God has established governmental authority for our good, and we are to obey it.

> Let every soul be subject to the governing authorities. For there is
> no authority except from God, and the authorities that exist are
> appointed by God. Therefore whoever resists the authority resists
> the ordinance of God, and those who resist will bring judgment on
> themselves (Rom. 13:1–2).

God is capable of executing His own judgment; it is not our job to
do so.

As a matter of principle, we are to obey the law; it is not a matter
of convenience. This includes obeying the fifty-five-miles-per-hour
speed limit. I would rather drive faster. But God's Word says we are
to "be subject to the governing authorities." This also includes all
the other laws and ordinances provided for our benefit. "Therefore
submit yourselves to every ordinance of man for the Lord's sake"
(1 Pet. 2:13).

We are reminded that the day of death, like the day of judgment,
cannot be avoided. Just as the unjust ruler cannot avoid judgment
of his evil actions, so he cannot avoid his own death. "There is no
discharge in that war" (v. 8). Wickedness may prevail in the affairs
of men, but it will do no good when the time of death is at hand.

There is another irony here. "There is a time in which one man
rules over another to his own hurt" (v. 9). In spite of a man's
inability to rule the number of his days, he still tries to "play God"
over the lives of others. The one who lords it over his subjects will
have to answer to the real Lord one day! Solomon's comment that he
has applied this principle "to every work that is done under the
sun" (v. 9) shows that this is God's verdict on all who deal unjustly
with those over whom they have authority. They do it to their own
hurt.

How should a Christian relate to all this? Solomon has answered
the question already in verse 1: We are to bless those who oppress
us. Our faces are to shine upon them!

Rather than complain bitterly about our high taxes (which are
low when compared to those of other Western nations), we are to
"do all things without murmuring and disputing, that . . . [we]
may become blameless and harmless, children of God without fault
in the midst of a crooked and perverse generation" (Phil. 2:14–15).
What a testimony that would be!

WHEN LIFE IS UNFAIR

If irritation with our leaders' abuses tops our list of complaints, injustice cannot be far behind.

> Then I saw the wicked buried, who had come and gone from the place of holiness, and they were forgotten in the city where they had so done. This also is vanity. Because the sentence against an evil work is not executed speedily, therefore the heart of the sons of men is fully set in them to do evil. Though a sinner does evil a hundred times, and his days are prolonged, yet I surely know that it will be well with those who fear God, who fear before Him. But it will not be well with the wicked; nor will he prolong his days, which are as a shadow, because he does not fear before God. There is a vanity which occurs on earth, that there are just men to whom it happens according to the work of the wicked; again, there are wicked men to whom it happens according to the work of the righteous. I said that this also is vanity. So I commended enjoyment, because a man has nothing better under the sun than to eat, drink, and be merry; for this will remain with him in his labor for the days of his life which God gives him under the sun (8:10–15).

It is important to remember that the context for these verses is the wicked rulers who have lorded it over their subjects. They continue to be honored, even in death! Perhaps those who continue to praise them have gained the most from the injustices they perpetrated, and they stand to gain from the continuation of those injustices. (The word "forgotten" in verse 10 probably should be translated as "praised," as in the RSV).

Solomon says, "I look at these wicked rulers who have done so many bad things to their people, and when it comes time for their funerals, they are praised in the very city where they did all their wickedness." So much for human acclaim! So much for justice!

Furthermore, because justice is not executed quickly, many people say, "Well, let's go ahead and do evil. If there was going to be any judgment, God or man or somebody would have done something by now!"

The psalmist struggled with the same problem:

Truly God is good to Israel,
To such as are pure in heart.
But as for me, my feet had almost stumbled;
My steps had nearly slipped.
For I was envious of the boastful,
When I saw the prosperity of the wicked (Ps. 73:1–3).

The psalmist goes on to talk about all the ways the wicked prosper; then he tells us he went off to worship God and was given an understanding of the actual consequences of their evil. "Surely You set them in slippery places;/You cast them down to destruction" (v. 18).

The psalmist could not understand the injustices in the world any more than we can. But he knew the character of God ("I have put my trust in the Lord God"—Ps. 73:28), and he knew that God would judge the evil ones. We can trust Him to do it, too.

It is easy to assume that because the administration of justice is slow it will never take place. It is not always possible to draw a direct line from an evil act to its judgment. Indeed, in our own time many people lament that the delay in administering justice has more to do with the breakdown of respect for the law than any other factor. Because God seems to delay His judgment, it is easy to assume that it will never come.

I remember my mother's telling a story in Sunday school when I was a child. A boy who was angry with his sister took her doll and buried it in the backyard. When his sister missed it and his mother asked him if he knew where it was, he denied having anything to do with its disappearance. Months later, when the grass began to grow in the spring, the doll was outlined on the bare ground and his lie was discovered.

When I was a little boy, I enjoyed playing with matches, even though I knew better. I would find a handful of matches, take them into my parents' clothes closet, shut the door, and light them one at a time. As each match burned out, I would put it in a neat little pile in the back of the closet. I never thought about being caught, but eventually I was.

I also disliked bread crusts. I would eat the soft part of the bread and would quietly slip the crust into the little drawer on my side of the kitchen table. For the life of me, I cannot imagine how I could have thought I would get by with it.

Of course, my wrong was discovered in that instance also. When we go against God's ways, there are always a stack of matches or a drawer full of bread crusts just waiting to be discovered.

It is just a matter of time.

The injustice of evil that goes unpunished is too much for Solomon, and he returns to the theme of judgment again: "It will be well with those who fear God. . . . It will not be well with the wicked" (vv. 12–13). But then he remembers the argument the secularist uses and acknowledges that this is not always true on this earth, "under the sun."

Sometimes the righteous suffer what ought to happen to the wicked, and the wicked enjoy what ought to go to the righteous. But whereas the unbeliever sees that as evidence that there is no God (or worse, even if there is one, then he is no god of mercy or is impotent), the person who lives by faith in the Lord God sees the issue differently.

Solomon has already declared, "I said in my heart, 'God shall judge the righteous and the wicked'" (3:17). At the end of the book he proclaims, "For God will bring every work into judgment, including every secret thing, whether it is good or whether it is evil" (12:14). So the believer knows that God is in charge, regardless of what may be happening at the moment.

Solomon's advice is delightfully simple: "So I commended enjoyment, because a man has nothing better under the sun than to eat, drink, and be merry; for this will remain with him in his labor for the days of his life which God gives him under the sun" (v. 15). It is as if Solomon was saying: "You say you're all bent out of shape because injustice exists? Are you wondering why God lets it continue? Are you wondering if He truly loves you or if He is able to do anything about it? Don't lose any sleep over the problem. Believe me. Enjoy yourself. That's what God wants you to do. He is in charge of running the world, not you."

Was Solomon oblivious to all the troubles of mankind? Hardly. He certainly could not have written this book without knowing the score in the game of life. He was simply reminding us of what we should have known all along: God is bigger than all of these things. Yes, He will mete out judgment. Yes, evil will be punished. In the meantime, enjoy your life.

Earlier in the book Solomon declared that enjoyment is from the hand of God (see 2:24–25). Then in chapter 5 he says, "It is good and fitting for one to eat and drink, and to enjoy the good of all his labor in which he toils under the sun all the days of his life which God gives him; for it is his heritage" (5:18). Here he again says we should enjoy life (see 8:15). In the next chapter, he will say it again, only in the imperative case: "Go, eat your bread with joy,/And drink your wine with a merry heart" (9:7).

God made us to enjoy life, and He commands us to do so. When we see the injustices that so irritate us, we need to cease our grumbling and remember that God is the judge of all mankind (see Rom. 12:19).

WHEN WISDOM IS NOT ENOUGH

At first glance, Solomon's advice is far too passive for our taste. It seems as if he is saying, "Well, if you can't lick 'em, join 'em." It is important to remember, however, that he has reminded us that our enjoyment of life is to be tasted alongside our work (v. 15). We are not to be passive, and presumably our "work" includes the pursuit of justice. Why else would God have instituted the governing authorities in the first place (see Rom. 13)? And the work of the governing authorities is done at times by Christians, too.

Solomon elaborates on his reason for advising us to enjoy our lives. We are unable to understand God's dealings, no matter how wise we are.

> When I applied my heart to know wisdom and to see the business that is done on earth, even though one sees no sleep day or night, then I saw all the work of God, that a man cannot find out the work that is done under the sun. For though a man labors to discover it, yet he will not find it; moreover, though a wise man attempts to know it, he will not be able to find it (8:16–17).

At first this seems discouraging; it is devastating to secular man. But if we will look closely at what he is saying, we will notice that Solomon intends it to be comforting. It is, after all, "the work of God" that we cannot understand. It is not the work of a cosmic madman, as some would say. Nor is it the blind chance the secularist sees at work in the universe. It is God's work.

And just as the tree in the Garden of Eden stood as a reminder that God has reserved some areas of knowledge for Himself, so these verses remind us again that we shall never discover those things He has chosen to keep secret (see Deut. 29:29; Is. 55:8–9).

All of us have inscrutable, uncomfortable experiences in our lives that we do not like and cannot understand. We read, "And we know that all things work together for good to those who love God, to those who are the called according to His purpose" (Rom. 8:28). When we read that, we sometimes wonder if it is really true.

But Solomon has told us what we need to know, and as he begins the next chapter he will review it with the words, "For I considered all this in my heart, so that I could declare it all: that the righteous and the wise and their works are in the hand of God" (9:1).

All that is left is to stand before Him and confess, with appropriate awe, the great affirmation of the apostle Paul:

Oh, the depth of the riches both of the wisdom and knowledge of God! How unsearchable are His judgments and His ways past finding out!

"For who has known the mind of the Lord?
Or who has become His counselor?"
"Or who has first given to Him
And it shall be repaid to him?"

For of Him and through Him and to Him are all things, to whom be glory forever. Amen (Rom. 11:33–36).

CHAPTER THIRTEEN

How Can I Find Joy in a World of Death?

Ecclesiastes 9:1–9

A friend recently shared a moving experience from the first church he pastored. Armed with his textbooks and the best knowledge his professors could pour into his head, he had entered the pastorate full of enthusiasm and hope for his ministry. The answers he had learned in seminary would handle every situation he would face.

And then Sandra Anderson died.

"It devastated me," he confided. "Things like that aren't supposed to happen. She was my age, beautiful, the mother of three small children, a committed Christian and wife. The all-American woman. One night she reached across the bed to wake her husband, Ralph, grabbed his shoulder violently, and then collapsed and died before he could get her to the hospital. Within minutes she had suffocated. The doctor said she had had a sudden allergic reaction to the penicillin she had been taking for a cold. Apparently, she had taken another pill only a few minutes earlier, and her body had decided it had had enough.

"I remember telling myself that this sort of thing just doesn't happen, at least not to committed people like Sandra and Ralph. The shock and desperation on Ralph's face and the confusion in their three children's eyes wouldn't leave my mind. I could hardly sleep, and I moved through all the things a pastor does at a time like that almost in a stupor.

"I was unprepared for what happened on the day of her funeral. I was a mess; but there was Ralph, comforting and encouraging the hundreds of family and neighbors and friends who had come to the funeral. It was as if he was the minister, not me.

"Later, I asked him about that day. 'How did you do it, Ralph?' I will never forget his answer.

" 'The night before the funeral, I took the kids over to my sister's place. I'd held my emotions in check, but I thought I was going mad and didn't want to hurt the children anymore or have them see me kill myself or something. When I got home, I began to weep. Uncontrollably. I just couldn't stop. Finally, I managed to crawl into bed, and I lay there all night, crying and clinging to Sandra's nightgown like Linus with his blanket. I could even smell her scent on the cloth. Then, near dawn, I began to realize that I wasn't alone in the room anymore. I began to feel a peace and quiet all around me. I'd never felt anything quite like it before, and a verse of the Bible came to my mind, "Lo, I am with you always" [Matt. 28:20]. It was like a voice. I knew that Jesus had come into that room to comfort me, and I knew I was going to be all right.'

"Ralph paused and wiped the tears from his eyes before going on. 'I'd been as low as I think I ever could go. I'd been hurt as deeply as anything could ever hurt me. And when I touched bottom, I discovered that what you and the other pastors of this church have always said was true. There was something there I could count on. Really Someone. I could rest on something solid. And I fell asleep.'

"'And when I woke up, everything was different. Oh, I was missing Sandra and it wasn't phoney or anything. But the Lord had given me a joy I couldn't understand. That wasn't me you saw that day. I'd been filled with unspeakable joy. It was Christ. That's who you saw.'"

How *do* we find joy in a world filled with death? With cruelty and suffering on every side? How can we talk about joy in that kind of world?

Recently I viewed the film *Joni,* the moving story of the young woman who was paralyzed from the neck down in a diving accident. Near the film's end, Joni made two profound assertions. She said there are a million questions, but only a couple of worthwhile answers. Also, there are a lot of *whys* she wonders about and does not understand, but she knows *Who* and that's enough.

How will we face the enigmas of life? So long as we focus our attention on the *whys,* we will be disturbed by them. In the last chapter we discovered that frequently the things that happen to the "good" people should be the things that happen to the "bad" people and vice versa, and in chapter 7 we learned that sometimes adversity is good for us and prosperity is bad for us. These teachings raise at least a million questions! And the more we try to understand, the more confused we become.

Solomon has an answer to these disturbing questions: Be joyful! But he wants to be sure we get his message in all its power, and so he takes us back to the rest of his argument again. He asks the secularist to look at life very carefully. If the believer will be equally honest, there will be some insights of great value for him also.

THE WORLD IS AN ENIGMA

It may seem strange to begin a discussion of joy in this way, but Solomon chooses to start us at the beginning of his thoughts.

> For I considered all this in my heart, so that I could declare it all: that the righteous and the wise and their works are in the hand of God. People know neither love nor hatred by anything that is before them (9:1).

According to the witness of Scripture, we should be able to see the hand of a mighty Creator in nature (see Ps. 19; Rom. 1:18–32). Even so, we have no objective way of knowing His attitude toward us: "People know neither love nor hatred by anything that is before them."

It is important to remember that Solomon is speaking from our perspective, that of mortal man. The one who lives "under the sun" is unable to tell by anything observable whether the God who made the sun is a god of love or hate.

Solomon has already made the point that the secular mind cannot be honest and come to any conclusion about life other than despair. Now he rubs it in. He says, "You don't even know what kind of a world this is, and you never will!" So long as people limit themselves to what they can observe—"by anything that is before them"—they will never understand the works of God.

But Solomon also said that "the righteous and the wise and their works are in the hand of God" (9:1). That is, God *is* a God of love, and He is in control.

People may not know this by what they observe in the world at large, but it is important to know that it is true. The believer— who has been made God's righteousness (2 Cor. 5:21)—can understand this, but the unbeliever cannot be consistent with his own "faith" and believe it. So these words—again—have a different meaning for the Christian than they have for the unbeliever. They are no cause for despair; God is known and His character is well-attested!

Solomon has already explained that we do not have the power to know what is good for us or what is evil (see 8:17). Here Solomon's words remind us that we do not know whether the things which come to us are God's blessing or His judgment. They could be either. There are times when it seems as if God is judging us, but the truth is that He has allowed it so that some good will take place in our lives.

Of course, it could be judgment, too! We do reap what we sow, and sometimes we simply suffer for our sin or stupidity. There is not much joy in that kind of suffering. It is foolish to step back and say, "I'm pressing on to higher ground," when we just dug ourselves a pit and fell into it!

But even in judgment God does not leave us. He teaches and corrects us. And in all troubled times there are lessons to learn. James wrote, "My brethren, count it all joy when you fall into various trials" (James 1:2). Why? "The testing of your faith produces patience. But let patience have its perfect work, that you may be perfect and complete, lacking nothing" (James 1:3–4). You see, God's ways are inscrutable. Sometimes we say, "Ah, now I know why such and such happened." But we probably do not! At best we see only a small fraction of God's purposes. Trials come for many reasons, and it is presumptuous for us to think we know more than we do.

Remember the story of Hosea. God told him to marry an immoral woman who was repeatedly unfaithful to him. Surely Hosea suffered greatly because of his wife's sin. But God commanded this so that Hosea might know how the Lord felt about the spiritual harlotry of Israel and might declare it with power and conviction. Hosea learned something, and the result was that the people were called to repentance.

On one occasion Jesus and His disciples came upon a man who had been blind from birth. Believing that such an unfortunate condition had to be a direct consequence of sin, they asked Him whether this man or his parents had committed a great sin. Jesus' comment was that neither case was true; it happened for the glory of God (see John 9:1–3). We, too, most likely have troubles that come our way so that God can be glorified. Do we allow them to glorify Him?

God wants us to grow, to stretch. He wants us to sink our roots deeper. It is in the time of drought that the plant sinks its roots farther into the soil. So it is with us.

Sometimes God wants us to suffer. We are called to suffer with Him: "But rejoice to the extent that you partake of Christ's sufferings, that when His glory is revealed, you may also be glad with exceeding joy" (1 Pet. 4:13). We are to know "the fellowship of His sufferings" (Phil. 3:10).

Granted, Christians in the United States do not suffer persecution as did the Christians of the early church and as Christians in Uganda, Cambodia, Viet Nam, Latin America, and numerous other countries suffer today. But I believe God designs special sufferings for each one of us so that we can grow in those areas that only these special sufferings allow.

But life is not filled only with enigmas and suffering. There is much more.

LIFE IS WORTH LIVING

We may not realize it while we are experiencing life's enigmas, but life is definitely of great value.

Everything occurs alike to all:
One event happens to the righteous and the wicked;
To the good, the clean, and the unclean;
To him who sacrifices and him who does not sacrifice.
As is the good, so is the sinner;
And he who takes an oath as he who fears an oath.

This is an evil in all that is done under the sun: that one thing happens to all. Truly the hearts of the sons of men are full of evil; madness is in their hearts while they live, and after that they go to the dead. But for him who is joined to all the living there is hope, for a living dog is better than a dead lion.
For the living know that they will die;
But the dead know nothing,

And they have no more reward,
For the memory of them is forgotten.
Also their love, their hatred, and their envy have now perished,
Nevermore will they have a share
In anything done under the sun (9:2–6).

"Everything occurs alike to all" (v. 2). We all die. As far as secular man is concerned, death is serious business. On the other hand, life is of inestimable value. It is so valuable that anything is better than death. "But for him who is joined to all the living there is hope, for a living dog is better than a dead lion" (9:4). In those days a dog was considered a despicable creature (see 1 Sam. 17:43; 24:14). The lion, however, has always been viewed as a beast of power, majesty, and grandeur.

Solomon was not giving advice on how to choose a household pet. He was simply saying that he would rather be a live dog—despicable as it was considered—than a dead lion—"the king of the jungle." Better to live than to die. Why? Because there is *hope* for the living. We have a similar expression: "Where there's life, there's hope." Life is precious. There need be no other reason.

But there is.

While there is life, there is a chance to prepare for death. There is a time to prepare to meet God. And when we die, there are no more opportunities to do anything worthwhile on earth.

Solomon is talking about mortal man and mortal life. Eternity is not in view when he says:

The dead know nothing,
And they have no more reward,
For the memory of them is forgotten,
And their love, their hatred,
    and their envy have now perished" (vv. 5–6).

He is talking about life "under the sun," life here and now. It is valuable; it is worth living.

LIFE IS A CAUSE FOR JOY

The ability to enjoy life is a *gift* to believers (see 2:25–26). It is not a possibility for unbelievers. It is sad that so often those who have the gift for enjoying life forget to use it. Yes, life has its enigmas, but we are commanded to enjoy it.

> Go, eat your bread with joy,
> And drink your wine with a merry heart;
> For God has already accepted your works.
> Let your garments always be white,
> And let your head lack no oil!

Live joyfully with the wife whom you love all the days of your vain life which He has given you under the sun, all your days of vanity; for that is your portion in life, and in the labor which you perform under the sun (9:7–9).

Notice the progression. In chapter 2, verses 24–26, Solomon recommends that we enjoy life. In chapter 3, verse 12, he says it again. In chapter 5, verse 18, he tells us it is our heritage. In chapter 8, verse 15, he commands that we enjoy life and here again in chapter 9 he tells us, "Live joyfully."

When Solomon speaks of bread and wine, he is talking about the staple diet of the time, a plain meal. We might say "meat and potatoes." The point is that we are to receive even the humble things in life with joy, not just the special things.

We have a simple rule at our house: We never take on heavy subjects while we are eating. We do not talk about the bills that are due, the energy crisis, the political scene, any dicipline or correction that needs to take place in our family, or problems from the church. We have the rest of the day to deal with those subjects. Meals are our time for positive, affirming, upbuilding talk—or silence. It is one way we try to communicate the joy of life to our children. Sometimes we parents have to go out of our way to make the point.

Not long ago I was speaking out of town, and a man I have known for twenty years came bounding up to me. "Bob," he exclaimed, "isn't it great how the Lord keeps us young and happy and rejoicing!" With an attitude like that, you might think he had the world by the tail. Not at all. For one thing, I wouldn't have his job for anything. I found myself warmed by his enthusiasm and love for the Lord as we talked, and I am convinced that his words did at least as much for me that day as mine did for him.

Do you know how to exude joy? Or do you concentrate on problems?

When Solomon refers to white garments and a well-oiled head, he is speaking of celebration—of a party. In those days the ordinary person wore cool, white garments for festive occasions only. He could not afford to keep them crisp and clean like the wealthy, who wore their white robes far more regularly. So the picture he paints is one of real rejoicing, a constant festive occasion. God wants our lives to be like a joyful party.

Even though he failed miserably in this area himself, he tells us that it is important for us to build joyful marriages. It is a part of what God intends for us to enjoy. We are not to become so enamored with our activities and work—including that which we do for the Lord—that we neglect the love of our youth. It is so important to nurture that love, to cultivate and enjoy that relationship. It is part of our portion in life. It is what God wants for us, and it should be one of the real highlights of daily life.

The price for a good marriage must be paid every day. There's an even higher price to pay when we will not pay the price to make marriage good.

We have not been given the answer to every question we can ask. There always will be enigmas, and in many cases we never will know the answers. But we are to refuse to allow them to rob us of the joy God wants us to have.

"This is the day which the LORD has made;
We will rejoice and be glad in it" (Ps. 118:24).

"The joy of the LORD is your strength" (Neh. 8:10).

Let us be sure that these words of Scripture become rooted deep in our souls.

CHAPTER FOURTEEN

How Should I Approach My Work?

Ecclesiastes 9:10–11:6

When life is over, what have I gained? What is my profit? Solomon personally faced these questions as he wrote the Book of Ecclesiastes. In the process of looking at life, he has shown us that we will not find satisfaction in knowledge, pleasure, or achievement—places where we normally look for it. Neither is it to be found in hard work or in wealth.

Life is full of harsh realities—injustice, death, oppression. It is filled with enigmas; we cannot really know whether something that happens to us is for good or for bad. What we feel is bad or unfair may turn out to be the best thing that ever happened to us.

So what shall we do? Do we give up? Do we become passive? Do we just go through the motions, doing enough to look good but not really having our hearts in it?

WORK ENERGETICALLY EVEN IF THE RESULTS ARE UNCERTAIN

When the granddaughter of the great conductor, Arturo Toscanini, was interviewed a few years ago, she was asked to identify the most important thing in her grandfather's life. Her response was surprising: Whatever he was doing at the moment! She went on to add that this was true whether he was peeling an orange or conducting a great symphony. The *important* thing was the thing he was doing.

Of course we can't all be Arturo Toscaninis, but regardless of our station in life, Solomon has provided us with valuable insights into our work—the tasks and concerns to which we give our energy, not just those things for which we are paid. Some of what he has to say is very clear and logical, while some of it is in loose collections of wise sayings, much as in the Proverbs.

Whatever your hand finds to do, do it with your might; for there is
no work or device or knowledge or wisdom in the grave where you
are going. I returned and saw under the sun that—

The race is not to the swift,
Nor the battle to the strong,
Nor bread to the wise,
Nor riches to men of understanding,
Nor favor to men of skill;
But time and chance
    happen to them all.
For man also does not know his time:
Like fish taken in a cruel net,
Like birds caught in a snare,
So the sons of men are snared in an
    evil time,
When it falls suddenly upon them (9:10–12).

We are to do what we do with our "might," whether it is peeling
an orange or directing a symphony, scrubbing floors or directing a
corporation. Whatever our tasks, we are to do them as unto the
Lord. Colossians 3:23 says something very similar: "And whatever
you do, do it heartily, as to the Lord and not to men." This
precludes the excuse, "Oh, if I were working for the Lord, it would
be different. But where I work, it doesn't make any difference."
    It does.
    We are to serve God in everything we do. Granted, while we
serve the Lord, we do serve people, too; but we must always remember that our real loyalty is to the Lord. We work enthusi-
astically, not as unto men, but as unto the Lord. When we help the
Red Cross or the Girl Scouts, we are to do it as unto the Lord.
    Someone has said, "Doing a little thing for God makes it a big
thing." So, "Whatever your hand finds to do, do it with your
might" (v. 10). Do it with energy! Do it with enthusiasm! It was
Thoreau who said, "None are so old as those who have outlived
enthusiasm." He was right.
    Solomon has already told us that life brings forces beyond our
control to bear upon us (see 3:1–8). We have only one life to make
our contribution; where we are going, there will be "no work or
device or knowledge or wisdom" (9:10). But in verses 11 and 12 we
begin to see the effects of both time and chance.

The fastest runner is not always the one who wins the race; the strongest warrior does not always win the battle (v. 11). Solomon could have had Samson in mind. Who was a mightier warrior than he, and yet who ever lost more? (His story is told in Judges 13–16.)

He could also have had his own father, David, in mind. When David was still a young man, he confronted the Philistine giant Goliath and declared, "You come to me with a sword, with a spear, and with a javelin. But I come to you in the name of the LORD of hosts" (1 Sam. 17:45). Who won? David, of course.

David's friend Jonathan faced the Philistines with only a handful of soldiers. As he led them into battle he declared, "Nothing restrains the LORD from saving by many or by few" (1 Sam. 14:6). The prophet Jeremiah explained why these apparent "upsets" in the natural order of things happen: "It is not in man who walks to direct his own steps" (Jer. 10:23).

GOD IS IN CONTROL, NOT MAN

Solomon has listed five assets that ought to guarantee success—speed, strength, wisdom, intelligence, skill. We would think that those who are quick, those who are strong, those who are wise, those who have intelligence, and those who know how to do things best would be the winners in life. Solomon says, "No, not necessarily. Man does not direct his own steps. There is a higher power—God."

The psalmist wrote that the person who walks with the Lord, who meditates on His Word, will be like the "tree planted by the rivers of water . . . whatever he does shall prosper" (Ps. 1:3). The Scriptures repeatedly declare that it is God who makes us prosper (see Gen. 39:3, 23; Deut. 29:9; 1 Kin. 22:15; 2 Chr. 26:5; Neh. 2:20; Ps. 122:6; etc.).

So as far as work is concerned, the results are not always certain. We do not know which races we will win and which battles we will be triumphant in. But God is at work; and because He is the one who directs man's steps, we ought to work with enthusiasm.

When Solomon ends his comments about the five assets that may turn out to be of little value, he says, "but time and chance happen to them all" (v. 11). No matter how much ability we have, time and chance take their toll.

Most of us are convinced that the opposite is true. We believe we are the masters of our fates, the captains of our souls. The secular mind is particularly insistent on this very point. "Not so," says Solomon. "For man also does not know his time:/Like fish taken in a cruel net,/Like birds caught in a snare,/So the sons of man are snared in an evil time,/When it falls suddenly upon them" (9:12).

Rather than the master of his fate, man is more like a little fish. He swims along minding his business, and suddenly he is snatched up by a net. There is nothing he can do about it. That image is the correct comparison for our lives, not this silly, vain talk about being masters and captains.

What will we do if a heart or lung fails us? What can we do if we contract a fatal disease? Not one thing! What can we do if we lose our job or our business? What will we do if a child dies or our spouse leaves us? How many times I have seen someone going along so well, and then—like a net scooping up a fish—it was all over.

Time and chance happen to everyone. We cannot predict what will happen to us or when it might occur. But regardless, we are to work with all our might. Solomon says, "Look, give it your best shot. Work with enthusiasm."

Ability is not as important as availability!

WORK WITH THE BENEFIT OF WISDOM

In another book Solomon wrote, "The fear of the LORD is the beginning of knowledge" (Prov. 1:7), and the Epistle of James reads, "If any of you lacks wisdom, let him ask of God" (James 1:5). Wisdom is a gift; God gives it. It is the ability to see things as God sees them. While we are to work with enthusiasm, we are also to work with wisdom.

> This wisdom I have also seen under the sun, and it seemed great to me: There was a little city with few men in it; and a great king came against it, besieged it, and built great snares around it. Now there was found in it a poor wise man, and he by his wisdom delivered the city. Yet no one remembered that same poor man. Then I said:
>
> "Wisdom is better than strength.
> Nevertheless the poor man's wisdom is despised,
> And his words are not heard.

Words of the wise, spoken quietly, should be heard
Rather than the shout of a ruler of fools.
Wisdom is better than weapons of war;
But one sinner destroys much good" (9:13–18).

At first glance it appears as if Solomon is saying it is foolish to be wise. A wise man delivers a city, but he is quickly forgotten and passes into oblivion. His point is that this is the gratitude one can expect for wisdom—it frequently goes unrewarded. It is good to realize that before we ask for it!

When Solomon declares, "Wisdom is better than weapons of war; but one sinner destroys much good" (9:18), he reminds us how valuable and vulnerable wisdom is. Wars could be avoided if we would live by wisdom, and it takes very little folly to destroy the fruits of wisdom.

This holds true in the arena of personal morality as much as in politics; how many have ruined their lives or reputations by one foolish action! The phrase, "One sinner destroys much good," is like our, "One rotten apple ruins the whole barrel." Why? The god of this world is Satan, and even a small effort from a sinner is met with an enthusiastic response.

Solomon amplifies these ideas in the following verses:

Dead flies putrefy the perfumer's ointment,
And cause it to give off a foul odor;
So does a little folly to one respected for wisdom and honor.
A wise man's heart is at his right hand,
But a fool's heart at his left.
Even when a fool walks along the way,
He lacks wisdom,
And he shows everyone that he is a fool (10:1-3).

It is easier to raise a stink than to create something beautiful! Some people seem to feel called to create problems. Their "little folly" frequently does far more damage than the good of many.

Verse two is not a political statement! Solomon simply says, "A wise man's heart inclines him to do what is right." *Left* and *right* are figurative expressions for "wrong" and "right," just as Jesus used the words *sheep* and *goats* to speak of those who follow Him and those who do not (Matt. 25:32).

Furthermore, the one distinguishing mark of the fool is that he cannot disguise what he is (see v. 3). His actions and his words—indeed, everything about him—show him to be the fool he is.

The wisdom literature of the Bible frequently comments on the fool. The Book of Proverbs speaks of him in many ways: Even when he says something right, it sounds wrong (see 17:7); it is wiser to avoid him (see 17:12); he loves to talk but does not listen (see 18:2); he is likely to cause conflict wherever he goes (see 18:6–7); his meddlesomeness is the cause of quarreling (see 20:3); honor does not fit his character (see 26:1); he is undependable (see 26:6–7). "Even a fool who keeps silent is considered wise; when he closes his lips, he is deemed intelligent" (17:28 RSV).

We have a similar expression, "Better to be thought a fool than to open your mouth and prove it."

WE ARE TO EXERCISE SELF-CONTROL

Solomon moves on to speak of our relationship with those with whom we work. His words apply equally well to our boss as to the political authorities.

If the spirit of the ruler rises against you,
Do not leave your post;
For conciliation pacifies great offenses.
There is an evil I have seen under the sun,
As an error proceeding from the ruler:
Folly is set in great dignity,
While the rich sit in a lowly place.
I have seen servants on horses,
While princes walk on the ground like servants (10:4–7).

The reason we are to be submissive to an unfair master is that his anger may be calmed by our own wise behavior. There is no benefit to be had in the anger of *two* people. Earlier, Solomon has written, "By long forbearance a ruler is persuaded," (Prov. 25:15) and "A soft answer turns away wrath,/But a harsh word stirs up anger" (Prov. 15:1). When one person is angry, the calm of another may restore a peaceable relationship. It works!

Furthermore, there is value in stable relationships. The reference in verse 7 to servants riding on horses and princes walking where servants would be expected to walk makes this very point. When errors of judgment are made, those who are inexperienced or incompetent are often admitted to positions of responsibility beyond their abilities; and everyone suffers. So when we are offended, we would be wise to swallow our pride and continue our work. If we indulge our self-righteousness and abandon our work, those who replace us may do a great deal of damage.

WORK WITH WISDOM

Solomon then proceeds to describe five situations in which wisdom has run amok and hurt has resulted from foolish actions:

> He who digs a pit will fall into it,
> And whoever breaks through a wall will be bitten by a serpent.
> He who quarries stones may be hurt by them,
> And he who splits wood may be endangered by it.
> If the ax is dull,
> And one does not sharpen the edge,
> Then he must use more strength;
> But wisdom brings success (10:8–10).

We ought to work with wisdom. The theme of the pit's becoming a trap to its maker is repeated frequently in Scripture (Ps. 7:15; 9:15; 35:7–8; 57:6; Prov. 26:27; 28:10).

The comment about the serpent's biting the one who leans against the wall (see also Amos 5:19) would be humorous in that culture. Since the walls were made of stones and everyone knew that snakes enjoy the cool shade and crevices that go with a stone wall, only a fool would casually lean against one without first checking it for snakes.

Furthermore, the careless person who quarries stones can easily be injured, and the one who splits wood carelessly can injure himself with the ax. Finally, the man who tries to cut wood with a dull ax has no one to blame for his misery but himself. He could make his work much easier, but instead he uses the dull blade and has to work much harder than necessary.

So wisdom is the difference between success and failure in our work. If we want success, we must use our God-given intelligence and do our work God's way.

LET YOUR WORDS GLORIFY GOD

A serpent may bite when it is not charmed;
The babbler is no different.
The words of a wise man's mouth are gracious,
But the lips of a fool shall swallow him up;
The words of his mouth begin with foolishness,
And the end of his talk is raving madness.
A fool also multiplies words.
No man knows what is to be;
Who can tell him what will be after him?
The labor of fools wearies them,
For they do not even know how to go to the city! (10:11–15).

In the first three lines of this Scripture passage, Solomon warns against stirring up "the babbler," the gossip, whom he compares to a dangerous snake. We all have known someone with a venomous tongue, and we know the damage loose talk can do. Solomon admonishes us to be circumspect in our speech when talking to such a person, lest we give him more fuel for his fire.

In contrast, think of the people you know with whom it is a blessing to talk. Their words are kind and helpful, winsome and warm. That kind of person's words help him; they are gracious. But a fool's words destroy him. He may appear as if he is doing all right until he speaks; then he reveals who he is and he's in trouble.

The fool's problem is not that he is slow-witted; one could hardly blame a person who is handicapped with low intelligence for his problem. No, the problem of the fool is that he thinks wrongly; he refuses to begin with God. Solomon says that he begins "with foolishness" when he speaks (v. 13); he has chosen to reject God, a judgment that should bring consternation to the secularist.

Solomon's point is that the one who lives without God does so deliberately. He has *chosen* to do so; he did not make his decision purely on the basis of objective evidence.

One writer comments, "If there are innumerable unbelievers whose earthly end could hardly be described as either wickedness or madness, it is only because the logic of their unbelief has not been followed through, thanks to the restraining grace of God."*

We already have seen that nobody knows what the future will bring (see 3:22; 6:12; 7:14; 8:7), but that does not deter the fool (v. 14). He will tell you what will happen, and in detail! Never mind the fact that he has even less reason to know than those to whom he speaks.

The comment in verse 15 is priceless: "The labor of fools wearies them, for they do not even know how to go to the city!" The fool is the kind of person who would get lost on an airplane! His whole orientation to life is so wrong that even ignorance cannot account for it; he contrives his lostness. He would make a straight road crooked; and even if he managed by chance to stumble upon the city, he would find a way to get lost in it!

A WORD TO THE WISE

Solomon has one final word to say about living and working wisely:

Woe to you, O land, when your king is a child,
And your princes feast in the morning!
Blessed are you, O land, when your king is the son of nobles,
And your princes feast at the proper time—
For strength and not for drunkenness!
Because of laziness the building decays,
And through idleness of hands the house leaks.
A feast is made for laughter,
And wine makes merry;
But money answers everything.
Do not curse the king,
    even in your thought;
Do not curse the rich,
    even in your bedroom;
For a bird of the air
    may carry your voice,
And a bird in flight
    may tell the matter (10:16–20).

*Derek Kidner, *A Time to Mourn, and a Time to Dance* (Downers Grove, Ill.: InterVarsity Press, 1976), p. 92.

We are affected by the tone set by those at the top of any organization. This is true of both good and bad leaders. Laziness, incompetence, or moral failure in any organization will cause it to collapse. This is true of nations, businesses, families. The word *child* in verse 16 may literally refer to a youthful leader, or it may refer to one who has inherited a position of responsibility without having to earn it. Either way, when an immature person rules an organization, it will be in trouble soon.

Solomon summarizes the philosophy of the childlike leader in verse 19: "A feast is made for laughter,/And wine makes merry;/But money answers everything." A fitting slogan for a fool!

The practical question is, "What shall I do when my boss is a fool?" Solomon warns us against stirring up opposition (see v. 20); a true fool will likely be vindictive, and those who have reached high places often have a sixth sense for knowing who their enemies are.

Recently, a friend who lived near Uganda during the rule of Idi Amin—its insane, cruel dictator—told me that Amin had a sense for knowing how to escape danger. Several attempts were made on his life, and each time he sensed something was wrong and took unusual precautions. Even at the end he managed to escape with his life.

The fool may be foolish, but he has a real knack for survival, warns Solomon. Be wise. Do your work well and wisely. Don't even think bad thoughts about your leaders.

Be gracious in your words. Work intelligently and wisely. Keep wisdom with you in all your work.

WORK ACTIVELY EVEN IF CONDITIONS ARE UNCERTAIN

As we work, it is wise to remember the realities of chapter 9, verses 11–12. We have no guarantees; time and chance can alter our best plans and destroy everything. While this is a disaster for the secularist, Solomon also intends for it to serve as a call to action for the believer. Since we have no guarantees for the future, it is better to risk following the Lord than to play it safe and withdraw from the activities of life.

> Cast your bread upon the waters,
> For you will find it after many days.
> Give a serving to seven, and also to eight,
> For you do not know what evil will be on the earth (11:1–2).

This is simply good advice; it makes sense. Since we cannot know when we will need help, it is wise to use our generosity to make as many friends as possible. Is this selfish? Not necessarily. If everyone would cast his "bread upon the waters," we would not need welfare or Social Security or any of the other expensive government programs that force us to do what we should gladly do on our own.

These words strike me as being very similar to Jesus' own words: "With the same measure you use, it will be measured back to you" (Matt. 7:2; see also Mark 4:24; Luke 6:38). "He who finds his life will lose it, and he who loses his life for My sake will find it" (Matt. 10:39; see also Luke 14:26; John 12:25).

This is a good way to work. It is a good way to live.

We ought to help those in need. I frequently hear people complain about those in need—the boat people, the poor, transients. "They're lazy." "Those foreigners will go on welfare if we bring them over here." "If we send food over there, the Russians may get hold of it and put their stamp on the packages." I would rather try to feed the hungry than worry about all the abuses that might happen and not try to feed them.

We comfortable Americans have become so insulated from the sufferings of people in other parts of the world that we fail to see the face of Christ in those who suffer. Instead, we think of the political advantages or disadvantages of helping them. It would be "better" to let the politicians—whose job it is to worry about politics—and the secularists—who really have no reason to help anyone in the first place—worry about all the reasons not to help those in need.

I have almost shuddered in my soul when Christians have been critical of feeding the hungry and destitute while we bring the gospel to them. When I hear those complaints, I frequently think of Solomon's words, "Whoever shuts his ears to the cry of the poor/ Will also cry himself and not be heard" (Prov. 21:13). We need to get busy feeding the hungry and clothing the naked and comforting the suffering.

Someday the tables could be turned.

REDEEM THE TIME

If the clouds are full of rain,
They empty themselves upon the earth;
And if a tree falls to the south or the north,
In the place where the tree falls, there it shall lie.
He who observes the wind will not sow,
And he who regards the clouds will not reap (11:3–4).

We need to distinguish between those things about which we can do nothing and those about which we can. We cannot stop nature's patterns; the rain will fall where it will, and the tree will fall where it will, too.

But we do not have to be passive. Solomon is saying, "So what if it isn't an ideal day to sow, and so what if it isn't ideal day to reap? If you wait for everything to be perfect, you will never do anything."

Our task in life is to deal with its realities the best we can. The conditions always could be better; but it is "better" for us to do our best with what we have than to wait for the perfect conditions, which may never come.

CONFIDENCE IS A PRODUCT OF FAITH

As you do not know what is the way of the wind,
Or how the bones grow in the womb of her who is with child,
So you do not know the works of God who makes all things.
In the morning sow your seed;
And in the evening do not withhold your hand;
For you do not know which will prosper,
Either this or that,
Or whether both alike will be good (11:5–6).

Finally, Solomon tells us why we can work with confidence in the midst of uncertainty. Those uncertain circumstances are in the hands "of God who makes all things" (v. 5). He not only created the physical world—the wind that blows—he also created mankind—the child that grows in its mother's womb.

This is the reason we should move ahead with our work (and by "work" I mean everything that occupies our creative and productive attention, not just our occupations). We do not know the consequences of the opportunities that come our way. We are not to wait until we know the results of our work before we take action, and we ought not be content to stay unemployed until the "perfect" job falls into our lap. Both are good formulas for failure. Rather, we are to get on with it. The work is ours; the result is God's.

The Scriptures say we are to redeem the time "because the days are evil" (Eph. 5:16). We do not know which of our actions will prosper and which will fail. Furthermore, even when we think something is a failure, it may actually be a success; and when we think something is a success, it may have been a failure (see 6:12).

A man recently told me of a friend of his whose commitment to the Lord was rather halfhearted. As they discussed their professions one day, his friend said, "Man, in my business the only thing that counts is profit. The only question I ask in getting into a deal is whether I can make a buck, and the faster the better."

My friend asked him if as a Christian he really believed that, but he did not push the point.

Several months later, his friend called him on the telephone and made an appointment for lunch. As they ate, he told an inspiring story. "You know, Ron, the craziest thing happened to me recently. I thought about that conversation we had several months ago and decided I would show you just how wrong you were and how stupid your question was. So I looked for the right opportunity to practice 'Christian love' in the business world.

"Sure enough, about a month-and-a-half ago I had a guy over the barrel. He had taken a gamble and had lost, and I could have forced him to live up to the letter of our agreement. Well, I wasn't real self-righteous about it or anything; but I explained that I had values other than just making an easy buck, and then I let him off the hook. It cost me about twenty thousand dollars off the bottom line to do it, but I gave him a break.

"You want to know something really crazy? I'd never been able to work with that guy. I couldn't even stand him. But in the last month he has given me more business than in the last five years, and I'm over a hundred thousand to the good, even counting the twenty I lost. We've even become friends."

We are told in the Scriptures to love our neighbor, to witness about Jesus Christ, to raise our children to love and fear the Lord, to be loyal and honest employees and employers, to give generously to those in need, as well as many other commands. We are not to wait for the ideal circumstances to begin to obey these commands. We are not to wait until their "success" is guaranteed, as though we are wise enough to know what success would be.

We are to get on with it.

"Whatever your hand finds to do, do it with your might" (9:10). Do it with energy. Do it with wisdom.

But do it.

CHAPTER FIFTEEN
How Can I Get the Most Out of My Life?

Ecclesiastes 11:7–12:14

Once we have explored the questions that matter, what profit is there? (see 1:3). This is the question Solomon repeatedly asks throughout the Book of Ecclesiastes. What profit is there in my life?

As we have looked at life with Solomon's assistance, we have seen that we do not find gain in the places people normally expect to find it. The reality of death changes every question; ultimately, there is no gain for man "under the sun." If there is to be any profit, it will have to come from something other than what we see; it will have to be a gift from God.

Interestingly enough, Solomon makes it a point several times to say, "Be sure you enjoy your life. That is what God wants for you, even though it has its limits and ultimately ends in death." Furthermore, "He has made everything beautiful in its time" (3:11). Everything fits together in God's plan—birth and death, happiness and sorrow, celebrating and mourning, gaining and losing. "He has put eternity into their hearts, except that no one can find out the work that God does from beginning to end" (3:11). We are pilgrims in this life, and we do not know all the answers to the questions we ask.

I am frequently asked by someone who is suffering, "Why do you think this happened?" I can only guess at the reasons and can truthfully answer, "Just like you, I don't know. But I know who does, and that's enough for me." He is a God of infinite, unending love. We can trust Him.

So we come through life with perhaps a million questions and only a couple of worthwhile answers, but they are enough. Who is in charge? God. What is He like? He's like a love beyond our fondest hopes! I rejoice in those two answers. I live in them by faith and hope.

It is from this perspective, then, that we should study Solomon's final words. We need to keep our eyes sharp and our hearts soft as we look for what God is saying through them.

ENJOY THE PRESENT WITH AN EYE
TO THE FUTURE

It is not easy for us to enjoy the present. When we are young, we tend to look forward to the future and say, "Oh, I wonder what it will be like! I'm really going to enjoy my life when I get older!" When we are older, it is tempting to look back on our earlier years and say, "Ah, those were the good days! How good they were, but how I wish I had put them to better use!" God doesn't want us to dwell on the past or daydream about the future; He wants us to find joy—through Him—in the present. So Solomon tells us, "Enjoy your life, but keep your eye on the future."

> Truly the light is sweet,
> And it is pleasant for the eyes to behold the sun;
> But if a man lives many years
> And rejoices in them all,
> Yet let him remember the days of darkness,
> For they will be many.
> All that is coming is vanity.
> Rejoice, O young man, in your youth,
> And let your heart cheer you in the days of your youth;
> Walk in the ways of your heart,
> And in the sight of your eyes;
> But know that for all these
> God will bring you into judgment.
> Therefore remove sorrow from your heart,
> And put away evil from your flesh,
> For childhood and youth are vanity (11:7–10).

Life is both delightful and serious. Its delights will last as long as we live, but not one moment longer. In the Scripture, "light" often is a synonym for "life." Its sweetness is to be enjoyed. When we are dead, we can no longer see the sun. That is, we will no longer enjoy "life under the sun."

We are to enjoy all our days, regardless of our age. But we are also to remember that the days of death—*darkness* is an image here for death—will be many. Death ushers us into eternity, and eternity is much longer than the few short years of our lives.

Solomon has wise advice for us in the days of our youth—enjoy yourself! He tells us to enjoy all the pleasures we can, but to remember that true joy will come from doing what is right. "But know that for all these God will bring you into judgment" (v. 9). The only thing God wants to take from us is emptiness, "vanity!"

Solomon is saying, "Live your life to the fullest. Enjoy your youth and get all the real joy you can. Just be sure to remember that someday you will give account of yourself to God. So pursue the innocent joys—the pure, godly, wholesome joys." The world will try to convince us that we are missing out on something, but we need to realize that the only things God would withhold from us are not worthwhile. Indeed, when we limit ourselves to the joys that are wholesome, we are free to do the things that actually bring joy, instead of guilt or regret. That lesson applies as well to adults as it does to youth.

When Solomon says, "Remove sorrow from your heart," he is telling us not to dread the loss of our youth while we should be enjoying it. It would be a disaster to miss the joy of our youth by fretting that some day we will no longer be young. Granted, the prospect of aging is terrifying for the secularist; but the Christian can see that every stage of life fits into God's good plan. It is good to be forty! So we are to live life to its fullest and live godly, holy lives.

LIVE FOR YOUR CREATOR DURING YOUR STRONGEST DAYS

This point grows quite naturally out of the first one. If we are going to live joyful, wholesome lives, then we ought to get busy now, while we have our greatest potential for joy.

Remember now your Creator in the days of your youth,
Before the difficult days come,
And the years draw near when you say,
"I have no pleasure in them":
While the sun and the light,
The moon and the stars,

Are not darkened,
And the clouds do not return after the rain (12:1–2).

To "remember" does not mean not to forget, or to jog one's memory. It is more like the story of God's remembering Hannah in chapter 1 of 1 Samuel. Hannah was barren and suffered tremendous embarrassment over it. Finally, in desperation she prayed for a child, and "the LORD remembered her" (v. 19).

Does this mean that God had been so preoccupied with something else that He had forgotten about Hannah's problem? No. It means He acted decisively on her behalf. When we "remember" God, we act decisively on His behalf; and when Solomon tells us to remember the Lord while we are young, he is telling us to consciously commit ourselves to serving Him. It is as if he is saying: "Begin to serve Him while you are enjoying your life to the fullest. Give your life to Him right now. Don't wait."

Live for your Creator during your strongest days!

The "difficult days" that come speak of the natural process of aging, in which our bodies begin to creak and groan and fall apart. It is amazing how quickly those days come! Someone said that getting older happens fast. "About the time your face clears up your mind gets fuzzy." Before we get to the stage where we say, "Boy, life sure isn't as much fun as it used to be," we ought to set our minds toward serving God with the best years of our lives. Through Solomon, God is saying, "Give me everything now. You will enjoy life more if you do, and you will be glad you did."

When he turns to describing the infirmities of old age, Solomon's words take on a somber tone. "The sun and the light, the moon and the stars" (v. 2) are all symbolic of joy. Our Creator wants us to delight in Him during the carefree days of our youth—the days when "the clouds do not return after the rain" (v. 2). He contrasts this stage of life with the "difficult days" of infirmity and old age, when one trouble comes upon the heels of another.

When we are young, we have the strength and resilience to overcome trouble; in our old age we will need every bit of strength we can find. It is better to face this while we are young and get on with living for God than it is to wait until all our strength is taken up with surviving and there is none left for serving the Lord.

REMEMBER GOD IN YOUR LAST DAYS

Verses 3 through 6 present an allegory in which Solomon compares an old, dilapidated house to our bodies as we age. He is not saying that all of these things happen to everybody. But it is an allegory that fittingly describes what we can expect in old age; and it should motivate us to serve God in our youth, whether our "youth" means our teens and twenties, or the "youth" of whatever years are left.

> In the day when the keepers of the house tremble,
> And the strong men bow down;
> When the grinders cease because they are few,
> And those that look through the windows grow dim;
> When the doors are shut in the streets,
> And the sound of grinding is low;
> When one rises up at the sound of a bird,
> And all the daughters of music are brought low;
> Also when they are afraid of height,
> And of terrors in the way;
> When the almond tree blossoms,
> The grasshopper is a burden,
> And desire fails.
> For man goes to his eternal home,
> And the mourners go about the streets.
> Remember your Creator before the silver cord is loosed,
> Or the golden bowl is broken,
> Or the pitcher shattered at the fountain,
> Or the wheel broken at the well.
> Then the dust will return to the earth as it was,
> And the spirit will return to God who gave it (12:3–7).

Each of these phrases is symbolic of some part of our bodies. "In the day when the keepers of the house tremble" refers to the arms and hands that begin to tremble from feebleness or palsy in old age. "And the strong men bow down" means that our legs become feeble and the knees begin to totter. "When the grinders cease because they are few" is a picture of our teeth, which become fewer in number. "And those that look through the windows grow dim" speaks of the eyes as they weaken and are less able to see, their pupils dilating less and becoming more contracted.

"When the doors are shut in the streets" refers to our lips. Because our teeth have fallen out, they are "shut" (a street is the area between two rows of houses). "And the sound of grinding is low" means that since we have so few teeth left, we cannot chew very well and need to trade in our Wheaties for oatmeal! "When one rises up at the sound of a bird" means that even the least amount of noise wakens you in the morning and you cannot get back to sleep. "And all the daughters of music are brought low" declares that our hearing lessens and our ability to make and enjoy music begins to escape us.

"When they are afraid of height" is a reference to the growing fear of falling, "and of terrors in the way" means that we begin to fear being jostled and injured as we move more slowly and un-steadily. "When the almond tree blossoms" refers to the hair turn-ing white, and "the grasshopper is a burden" alludes to the halting walk of the elderly as they go on their way. "And desire fails" suggests that both sexual desire and power are lost. "For man goes to his eternal home, and the mourners go about the streets" warns of one's impending death and the mourning that will accompany the funeral.

"Remember your Creator before the silver cord is loosed, or the golden bowl is broken" could refer to the spinal cord and the brain; or it could refer to the fragile quality of life (much like a beautiful, golden lamp bowl suspended by a fine silver chain), which can be ended with a snap. The "pitcher shattered at the fountain" is a figure of speech for the heart, and "the wheel broken at the well" speaks of the veins and arteries that carry the blood throughout the body like a water wheel.

"Then the dust will return to the earth" reminds us of God's words to Adam: "For dust you are, and to dust you shall return" (Gen. 3:19). The spirit's returning "to God who gave it" reminds us of the source of our life (see Gen. 2:7).

Solomon says, "Now, before these things happen—and you can be sure that at least some of them will—live for the Lord. Give Him the strength of your strongest days. Use them for God. Don't just give Him what little is left over after you have wasted your strength."

Old age is a marvelous experience of its own, and I do not believe Solomon intends to ridicule it with his vivid word pictures. When a person has lived for God all his or her days, old age can be a glorious time; but it will not be a time of strenuous service for God.

So if we are going to serve the Lord, we must do what we can while we can!

FEAR GOD AND KEEP HIS COMMANDMENTS

This is the conclusion to everything that has been written:

> "Vanity of vanities," says the Preacher,
> "All is vanity."
>
> And moreover, because the Preacher was wise, he still taught the people knowledge; yes, he pondered and sought out and set in order many proverbs. The Preacher sought to find acceptable words; and what was written was upright—words of truth. The words of the wise are like goads, and the words of scholars are like well-driven nails, given by one Shepherd. And further, my son, be admonished by these. Of making many books there is no end, and much study is wearisome to the flesh (12:8–12).

Again the Preacher returns to his thesis: "All is vanity." One could argue for including it in the previous section, but I have included it here because it serves as a reminder of Solomon's verdict on all the areas in which humans strive. In the end, all human effort is worthless, futile. It is only in that context, then, that we are ready to hear Solomon's conclusion.

In calling himself wise, Solomon was referring to the three great religious institutions of his day—the prophets, the priests, and the wise men. He was not being egotistical. A "wise man" was designated as such in recognition of God's gifting him with wisdom, much as we ordain ministers in recognition of God's calling them to ministry.

These sayings serve two purposes. Two images illustrate them—

the goad and the nail. The goad was a long stick with an iron point which was used to prod oxen into doing something, or at least doing it faster. Solomon's words are to prod us into action; they are not written for armchair Christians. If we take God's Word and live according to it, we let it be a goad in our lives.

In Solomon's day nails were used for different purposes than we use them for today. They were used to fasten tents securely to the ground so that when the wind and rain came, they would be secured firmly. Obviously, these nails were much larger than ours; they were more like stakes.

Solomon's point is that the Word of God is like a nail that holds your life safe and secure. When you know the Word of God, you can hang great weight upon it; it is strong and secure. So the Word of God is like a nail, in that it gives focus to our lives and provides us with security.

Therefore, the Word of God prods us to service, and it is our protection. The goads and nails are given by Jesus Christ, the "one Shepherd" (v. 11).

We are warned that all we need is Solomon's words. Some translations are more pointed: "My son, beware of anything beyond these" (v. 12, RSV).

"Of making many books there is no end, and much study is wearisome to the flesh" (v. 12). This does not mean we should not study; rather, when we wrestle with life's hard questions, we are to take God's Word as the answer. Solomon is saying: "Take the Word of God and believe it. Where God has put a period, don't you put a question mark. Don't be caught up in endless searching, but come to the truth."

Having informed us of the value of his words and of the danger of not taking them seriously, Solomon now states the truth that caused him to write his book. Up to now everything has fallen short of clearly stating what these verses contain. There have been hints and foreshadowings of their truth; here we see it clearly and forcefully.

Let us hear the conclusion of the whole matter:

Fear God and keep His commandments,
For this is the whole duty of man.

For God will bring every work into judgment,
Including every secret thing,
Whether it is good or whether it is evil (12:13–14).

In contrast to the "vanity" that has permeated Ecclesiastes, we are finally presented with that which is not vain: "Fear God and keep His commandments." When we fear God, it puts us into a proper relationship with Him. It is not so much a matter of fear in the sense of terror as it is of fear in the sense of awe. To fear God is to hold Him in awe, to reverence Him. If we do so, it will affect everything we do or think. It will cause us to understand and accept our proper place in the universe and will keep us from thinking higher of ourselves than we should. Only this way can we escape the folly of the secularist who says "There is no God" (Ps. 14:1).

When we keep God's commandments, we live consistently with what God has made us to be. I think we often confuse keeping God's commandments with legalism, obeying a list of rules that tell us what we can and cannot do. Instead, we ought to view it as following the plan God mapped out for us in all His magnificent love. He knows what we need; He created us. He loves us, and His commandments are for our good. "Oh, how I love Your law!" (Ps. 119:97).

It is comforting to know that "God will bring every work into judgment" (12:14). If God is concerned enough about me to pass judgment on my life, then ultimately everything in it has value. None of it is vain, or meaningless.

This is the catch. Wise man that he is, Solomon has painted us into a corner. All along he has teased us—and especially those who ignore the Lord—with the fear that nothing has any value, that nothing has any meaning whatsoever. The secularist has had to go along with Solomon's argument. What basis would he have for arguing with him?

Now, here, finally—at "the conclusion of the whole matter"—Solomon proclaims the truth: God *is* going to pass judgment on our lives. This means that everything is vitally important. Nothing in my life goes unnoticed, much less all of it!

It is a marvelous, joyous, and wonderful truth. The Creator and King of all creation takes us very seriously.

Ultimately, then, the meaning of life turns on this very question. Is it for nothing? Or is it of priceless value?

Solomon has given his answer. You will give yours by the choices you make.